Foreword by Lord Sainsbury of Turville

As this report clearly shows, the performance of UK universities in knowledge transfer has dramatically improved in the last ten years and now compares favourably with universities in the United States. Not only have our world-class research universities maintained their outstanding record of research, but they are now producing a high level of patents, licensing agreements, industrial research and spin-off companies. Also around many of them, as the report vividly describes, high-tech clusters are growing up. These not only provide the knowledge and information-rich conditions which spin-off companies need to grow and be profitable but also attract spin-in companies and foreign research institutes.

It has been claimed that industrially we live on a 'flat earth' where geography is no longer important and where talented individuals across the world compete on a level playing field. But the reality is different. In the new global economy if high-tech companies want to be competitive, they need to locate the key parts of their operations in knowledge and information-rich regions where there is a concentration of the research, creative individuals and infrastructure needed for innovation. And the government must adopt the policies which enable such clusters to grow and be successful.

At a time when the UK needs to look for new sources of growth, providing the right conditions for high-tech manufacturing companies and knowledge-intensive business services should be a priority, and there is an exciting opportunity for government and RDAs to build on the success that has already been achieved.

As the report makes clear our world-class research universities are already having a major economic impact on their surrounding areas. This should not come as a surprise. If one looks at the USA one finds that the universities which have had most impact on their local economies, such as MIT, Berkeley, Stanford and Austin, are all world-class research universities.

There is, however, enormous scope for business-facing universities to more actively engage with small- and medium-sized businesses in their regions, and government and the RDAs should make certain that they have the incentives and resources to do so. Also a few tentative initiatives have been taken in supporting knowledge transfer from FE colleges and this is something that government and RDAs ought now to be rapidly expanding. For many small businesses the best organisations to help them be more innovative and profitable will be FE colleges rather than universities.

At a time when it is essential to produce the best possible conditions for high-tech manufacturing to grow and be profitable, there is a danger that a great deal of effort will be wasted in introducing totally new incentives or policies. Instead of doing so, the most valuable action that government and the RDAs could take, as this report makes clear, is to build on what has been achieved in the last 15 years and to encourage universities to travel further along the exciting road on which they have already embarked.

It is not possible to predict exactly where new jobs will emerge in the future, but it is possible to see many opportunities for UK industries to create new products and services, and new industries, in areas as diverse as aerospace, pharmaceuticals, biotechnology, regenerative medicine, telemedicine, nanotechnology, the space industry, intelligent transport systems, new sources of energy, creative industries, computer games, business services, computer services and education. We can also be certain that many of the new businesses which will drive change in these industries will be developed in the high-tech clusters around our universities.

Lord Sainsbury of Turville
April, 2009

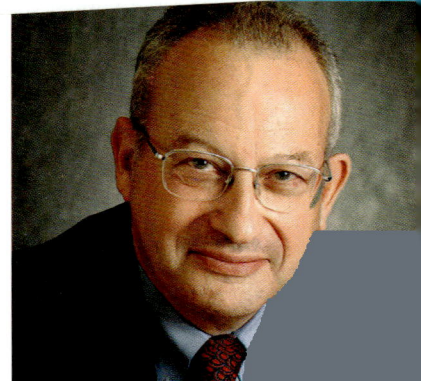

Executive summary

The UK's universities are precious national assets, regularly leading the world in the quality of their research and discoveries. But for decades, policymakers have wrestled with the question of how to turn academic excellence into economic impact. With the collapse of the UK's financial services sector, this issue has become urgent. The innovative businesses that our universities create and support will be essential to allowing us to emerge strongly from the recession. This report asks how we can make this a reality.

It begins by examining the multifaceted contribution that universities make to the economy, highlighting their importance as sources of knowledge, and also their role as sources of skilled employees and as the centres for regional economic clusters.

Eight case studies show how thriving clusters of economic activity have grown up around leading UK universities, and the effect of recent policy and university strategy in helping this to happen.

The case studies also show that the way universities interact with businesses is evolving. The earliest collaborations, such as those seen in the initial growth of the Cambridge cluster, relied significantly on good fortune and often happened below the university's radar, a model we have called the 'serendipitous university'. Over the past 15 years, the process of formal knowledge transfer – developing spin-out companies, profiting from patents and licences – has been professionalised and upgraded. This 'commercial university' model has helped promising clusters emerge more widely. More recently, universities have been casting their attention even more broadly, thinking not just about the formal transfer of intellectual property to industry, but also their role in building clusters, connecting to the national and international economies and bringing together thinking, practice, and finance. This

model of the 'connected university' holds the key to further economic growth.

Building the links to encourage business growth will become an increasingly urgent issue for universities. As public sector funding in other areas is cut, there will be an increasing onus on universities to demonstrate the public and economic benefit of spending on science, technology and research. There are several ways that universities can do this:

- Getting the basics right: ensuring that technology transfer organisations are performing at the standard set by leading UK institutions; or good practice initiatives in the wider pool of pre- and post-1992 institutions.

- Embracing the model of the 'Connected University': recognising the importance of building networks with local firms, nurturing local clusters, creating national and international connections, and putting this at the heart of their strategy.

- Recruiting, developing and promoting more 'boundary spanners': people whose experience encompasses both public and private sectors who can build links between them.

- Measuring the benefits of university-business interaction more effectively and communicating these to the public.

Government has a role to play as well. Local government should look carefully at how it applies planning regulations to universities. Since physical spaces for university-business interactions are just as important as institutions, local authorities interested in innovation and growth should give priority to requests to develop places where firms and universities can interact. Local authorities and universities should move beyond a transactional relationship focusing on planning, to a broader dialogue on the role the university can play in local economic development.

The funding system should also take into account the importance of university-business interaction. Those portions of university funding dedicated to encouraging universities to interact with the outside world – such as the Higher Education Innovation Fund (HEIF) – should better measure the contributions that universities make to the local, national and international economies, to sharpen the incentives for co-operation. A version of HEIF should be extended to the Further Education Sector. The forthcoming Research Excellence Framework should increase the rewards for interdisciplinary and outward-facing research, drawing on existing good practice among research councils.

The recession presents a unique chance for us to realise the economic benefits of our first-class research base. This is an opportunity that the UK cannot afford to miss.[1]

1. Parts of this report draw on research supported by the Economic and Social Research Council (grants RES-171-25-0018 and RES 171 25-0038). The usual disclaimer applies.

Acknowledgements

The authors would like to thank: Dr Ronnie Ramlogan, Emeritus Professor John Goddard, Professor Colin Whitehouse, John Leake, Dr Paul Treloar, Andy Sharp, Linda Enderby, Professor Bill Wakeham, Dr Tony Raven, Emma Connolly, Graeme Purdy, John Dersley, Alan Sanderson, Professor Ian Clarke, Davide Consoli, Dimitri Gagliardi, Alice Frost, Adrian Day, Matt Hatch, Simon Bond, Andy Curtis, James Bates, Professor Philip Jones, Professor Mike Smith, Iain Wilcock, George Whitehead, Dr Ivan Griffin, Libby Kinsey, Andrew Small and Alex Hook.

NESTA is the National Endowment for Science, Technology and the Arts.

Our aim is to transform the UK's capacity for innovation. We invest in early-stage companies, inform innovation policy and encourage a culture that helps innovation to flourish.

Contents

The Connected University
Recovery and Growth in the UK Economy

2. Times Higher Education, World University Rankings 2008. See http://www.timeshighereducation.co.uk/hybrid.asp?typeCode=243&pubCode=1&navcode=137

3. Evidence (2008) 'International comparative performance of the UK research base.' Report to the Department for Innovation, Universities and Skills. London: DIUS.

4. Consider, for example, the role of universities in enabling the growth of 'phoenix industries' in areas of industrial decay. See Christopherson, S. and Clark, J. (2009) 'Remaking regional economies.' New York: Routledge.

5. HM Treasury (2008) 'Pre-Budget Report.' London: HM Treasury.

6. It should be acknowledged here that the term 'cluster' is a much-contested term and has been variously defined. Clusters in this report are defined as geographically proximate concentrations of interconnected firms, including specialised suppliers and related service providers and innovation intermediaries, as well as other key institutions, notably here, universities, which co-operate (and compete) usually in a particular set of technologies linked by a set of commonalities and complementarities. Clusters should be seen as directly bestowing certain economic benefits to firms and other organisations in the cluster and potentially indirectly to other firms and actors in the cluster locality through spillover and other benefits. They should be seen as therefore more than just simple concentrations or agglomerations of firms and other economic actors in an area. The geographic scale of these clusters can range from a city or region through to inter-regional or international scales of collaboration and networking.

7. Swann, G. (2006) Universities and Business Innovation. In: DTI (2006) 'Innovation in the UK: Indicators and Insights.' DTI Occasional Paper No. 6. London: DTI.

8. Lester, R. (2005) 'Universities, Innovation, and the Competitiveness of Local Economies: A Summary Report from the Local Innovation Systems Project—Phase I.' MIT Industrial Performance Center Working Paper 05-010. Cambridge, MA: MIT.

9. Stone, I. et al. (Eds) (1997) 'Northern Economic Review.' Issue 26. Newcastle: Northern Economic Research Unit, University of Northumbria at Newcastle.

Part 1: Universities have a vital place in the knowledge economy

The UK's research universities are one of its success stories. The UK has four universities in the top ten of the world – the only top-ten universities outside the United States.[2] UK researchers are the most efficient and productive in the world and our research base is second only to that of the US in terms of most leading scientific indicators.[3] Our research excellence has not, however, been accompanied by the kind of economic success we associate with the US's technology sector. Addressing this question has been a core goal of UK science and innovation policy in recent years.

The importance of translating our research excellence into economic reality has been brought into sharp focus by the financial crisis and the ensuing global recession. At a national level, the recession makes urgent the need to find new sources of economic activity to take the place of financial and business services and drive future growth. At a regional level, universities are often the most stable and permanent feature of local economies that may otherwise be buffeted by unemployment, business failure, and corporate retrenchment; effective engagement between a local university and local businesses can mean the difference between local decline and local resilience.[4]

The strength of the higher education system will be tested by the current economic crisis – but also its importance is likely to increase after the crisis has subsided. According to the Treasury the current crisis will cause a permanent 5 per cent reduction in GDP.[5] Following the severe recession of the early 1980s, lost manufacturing output was compensated for by the growth of financial services; the issue now is what will make up

for the sharp contraction in financial services? The higher education system has an important role to play here, because it is a sector where the UK has a strong competitive advantage, because it is more resilient to business cycles and economic shocks than many other parts of the economy, and because it offers a feedstock of skills and knowledge for new and established businesses to drive innovation and growth.

This report asks how this growth comes about, and how to make it more likely. First of all, it examines the different way in which universities support economic growth, based on practical examples and the extensive academic literature on the subject. Second, it looks at a series of case studies of UK universities that have generated thriving clusters of economic activity around them.[6] Finally, it draws conclusions from these case studies about how universities' interaction with businesses and society is developing, and how policy can help translate our research excellence into economic growth.

Universities are powerful economic actors with four important roles

Universities contribute to the economy in several ways. Their most celebrated role is as well-springs of discoveries, ideas and technologies, some of which have great commercial value. But their other functions are also important, not least because of their stability and permanence. Universities act as significant employers and purchasers in many areas. They produce a skilled workforce that is often a crucial resource for local businesses. And, more subtly, they provide a locus for co-ordinating local activity, benefiting local firms both through the informal exchange of knowledge and expertise, and by offering an anchor around which regional clusters can form. The academic literature suggests that collaboration between businesses and universities is associated with improved business performance across a range of indicators, including new market entrance and increased market share; production of an increased range of goods or services; producing higher quality goods or services; and generating higher value added.[7]

Universities are especially important to local economies because of their stability

The ongoing effects of globalisation and the immediate challenges of the recession are making key economic actors more mobile: firms move in response to shifts in comparative advantage or recessionary pressures; and workers, particularly those that are skilled, move in response to differences in wages and the quality of life. This mobility of the factors of production may improve the efficiency of markets but it can put severe strain on places that lose businesses or workers. Places need embedded economic actors – and universities are one of the most important. They may expand or decline, but they rarely go elsewhere.[8] Although the benefits of a great research university may be felt worldwide, they are at the same time uniquely important local institutions. We now consider the specific ways in which universities can benefit their localities.

1. Universities are important sources of local employment and purchases from local suppliers

The most direct effect universities have on their localities is by increasing local demand. The expenditure impact of universities comprises the direct and indirect jobs created; as well as the extra income within an economy that a university generates. The economic 'multiplier effect' of a university is greater than that of most private sector firms because of the structure of turnover, and the proportion of expenditure by staff and students likely to remain in the local area.[9] A number of studies on the local impact of university expenditure in various parts of the UK find significant income effects due to staff salaries and goods and services together with spending by students; they also find that increases in income in the regions generate a multiplier effect which feeds its way through a number of sequential rounds of expenditure.[10] Additionally, the growth of universities may have positive impacts on the built environment as new buildings and facilities often replace derelict industrial, residential or commercial areas.[11]

Consider for example the direct economic effects of the University of Cambridge, which as of 2006 employed more than 11,700 people directly and indirectly supported more than 77,000 jobs in the Eastern region.[12] It was estimated at the time that if the university did not exist, the economic impact on the UK economy between 2006 and 2016 would be a £4.4 billion loss in GDP and approximately 10,800 fewer jobs, and the impact on the region would be even greater, "requiring replacement of a net present value of £21.2 billion in GDP".[13] This excludes the importance of the technology cluster associated with the university.

2. Universities produce skilled workforces and transfer knowledge through their graduates

National and local economies benefit from having graduates – and this exceeds the impact of those with a university education normally having a relatively high income. (Graduates receive an annual average wage 16 to 20 per cent higher than individuals with A-level qualifications, although there is significant variation by subject and place of study.)[14] The transfer of graduates is a highly effective method of knowledge exchange, not least because much of the most important knowledge is tacit, which is exchanged through informal interactions rather than codified knowledge which can be transferred through less personal mechanisms.

Universities' role in building regions' human capital also increases their social capital,[15] a concept that encompasses trust, network and community engagement. A high level of social capital generates a number of economic and social benefits over and above the direct impact of a more skilled workforce.[16] For instance, mutual trust aids the transfer of knowledge and it reduces transaction costs, as those who trust one another are less likely to need expensive contracts to interact with one another. And those that are most trusting – and trust others from different social, economic and ethnic backgrounds – are those with the highest level of education.[17]

10. Studies include:
    Nottingham: See Bleaney, M., Binks, M., Greenaway, D., Reed, G. and Whynes, D. (1992) What does a University add to its local economy? 'Applied Economics.' 24, pp.305–311.
    Greater Manchester: See Robson, B., Deas, I., Topham, N. and Twomey, J. (1995) 'The economic and social impact of Greater Manchester's Universities.' Manchester: Centre for Urban Policy Studies, University of Manchester and Salford University Business Services Ltd.
    Newcastle: See Lincoln, I., Stone, I. and Walker, A. (1995) The Contribution of Newcastle's Higher Education Sector to the Local Economy. 'Northern Economic Review.' 1995, Issue 24.
    Birmingham: See Centre for Urban and Regional Studies/GHK (2007) 'Regional and Local Impact Assessment of the University of Birmingham Centre for Urban and Regional Studies.' Birmingham: University of Birmingham.
    Bournemouth and the South West: See Fletcher, J. and Morakabati, Y. (2007) 'Bournemouth University Economic Impact Study, 2007.' Bournemouth: University of Bournemouth.

11. Building Futures (2009) 'Growing by Degrees: Universities in the Future of Urban Development.' London: Royal Institute of British Architects.

12. The University includes the Faculties, Colleges, Cambridge University Press and Cambridge Assessment.

13. Library House (2006) 'Cambridge Cluster Report 2006.' Cambridge: Library House.

14. Warwick University (2009) 'Returns to higher education: variations by subject and degree class.' Warwick: Warwick Economics Department, Warwick University. Available at: http://www2.warwick.ac.uk/fac/soc/economics/research/centres/eri/bulletin/2008-09-2/naylor/

15. Iyer, S., Kitson, M. and Toh, B. (2005) Social capital, economic growth and regional development. 'Regional Studies.' 39, pp.1015–1040.

16. Putnam, Robert D. (2007) E Pluribus Unum: Diversity and Community in the Twenty-first Century. The 2006 Johan Skytte Prize Lecture. 'Scandinavian Political Studies.' 30:22, pp.137–174.

17. Iyer, S., Kitson, M. and Toh, B. (2005) Social capital, economic growth and regional development. 'Regional Studies.' 39, pp.1015–1040.

18. See HM Treasury Annual Report for each year, 2005 to 2008. HM Treasury (2008) 'The ten-year science and innovation investment framework annual report.' London: HM Treasury.

19. HEFCE (2008) 'Higher education-business and community interaction survey: 2006–07.' Available at: http://www.hefce.ac.uk/pubs/hefce/2008/08_22/

20. Chesbrough, H. (2003) 'Open Innovation: The New Imperative for Creating and Profiting from Technology.' Cambridge, MA: Harvard Business School Press, Harvard University.

21. Laursen, K. and Salter, A. (2004) Searching high and low: what types of firms use universities as a source of innovation? 'Research Policy.' 33:8, pp.1201-1215.

22. The dynamics of university-industry links have generally been analysed from the point of view of:

The firm: See Laursen, K. and Salter, A. (2004) Searching high and low: what types of firms use universities as a source of innovation? 'Research Policy.' 33:8, pp.1201-1215.

Particular sectors or clusters: See Meyer-Krahmer, F. and Schmoch, U. (1998) Science-based technologies: university-industry interactions in four fields. 'Research Policy.' 27, pp.835-851.

Individual scientists: See D'Este, P. and Patel, P. (2007) University-industry linkages in the UK: what are the factors underlying the variety of interactions with industry? 'Research Policy.' 36:9, pp.1295-313.

Technology transfer organisations: See Bercovitz, J. et al. (2001) Organizational Structure as a Determinant of Academic Patent and Licensing Behavior: An Exploratory Study of Duke, Johns Hopkins and Pennsylvania State Universities. 'The Journal of Technology Transfer.' 26:1, pp.21-35.

Some studies have focused on both the university and the firm side. See Charles, D. and Howells, J. (1992) 'Technology Transfer in Europe: Public and Private Networks.' London: Belhaven Press.

Others explore the nature and dynamics of collaborative projects. See Carayol, N. (2003) Objectives, agreements and matching in science-industry collaborations: reassembling the pieces of the puzzle. 'Research Policy.' 32:6, pp.887-908.

Studies have mainly relied on surveys on university industry links. See Cosh, A., Hughes, A. and Lester, R. (2006) 'UK plc: Just

3. Universities are leading sources of knowledge

The 1993 White Paper 'Realising Our Potential' highlighted the importance of academic research in generating wealth and improving the quality of life. The role of universities as an important part of the innovation ecosystem has been emphasised by the Lambert review of university-business collaboration in 2003, the Sainsbury review of government's science and innovation policies in 2007, and has been reinforced in a series of reviews on the science and innovation framework 2004-2014.[18]

A common view of how university knowledge contributes to economic growth centres around the commercialisation of this knowledge by businesses. Central to this view are the concepts of intellectual property, which generates licensing revenue and wealth from spin-outs, and know-how, which generates consulting and advisory services. For example, Cambridge, at the forefront of university-business interaction in 2006/07, filed 112 patents, generated 35 licences, increased its overall portfolio of active spin-outs to 45 and generated income of almost £3.5 million from intellectual property.[19]

The increasing importance of the 'open innovation' model – involving interactions between different businesses and other firms and organisations such as universities rather than a reliance on proprietary in-house research and development (R&D) – increases the significance of university-business links in the innovation process. The open innovation model relies on letting ideas flow into a business to improve innovation and business performance, rather than relying on in-house R&D.[20] Research indicates that firms that adopt open innovation strategies and invest in R&D are more likely than others to use knowledge from universities.[21]

Recent research shows that formal technology transfer is only part of the picture.[22] Indeed, for the majority of firms, universities are most important not as sources of intellectual property, but for other types of knowledge that are harder to package up and codify. One recent survey, the results of which are shown in Table 1, highlights the importance to businesses of 'assistance in problem solving' and 'improving understanding', which are more readily gained through consulting or through informal interactions than by traditional spin-outs or licensing.

Data from the Higher Education-Business and Community Interaction survey also suggest that revenues from technology transfer account for only a small share of the income UK universities make from their knowledge, with paid research and consultancy significantly more important (see Figure 1). This holds true even among the most elite research institutions. Case studies

Table 1: Benefits reported by firms from interactions with universities

Benefits from interactions with university	Percentage of firms
Assistance in problem solving	67.3
Improve understanding	66.7
Sources of information for new projects	57.5
Recruitment of postgraduates	42.0
Downstream-related activities	29.3
Training of company employees	27.4
Generation of patents	20.0

Source: D'Este, P. (2008).'Gaining from Interactions with University: Multiple Methods for Nurturing Absorptive Capacity.' Paper presented at the DRUID Conference on Entrepreneurship and Innovation – Organizations, Systems and Regions, Copenhagen, Denmark, June, 2008.

Figure 1: UK universities' income from business interaction

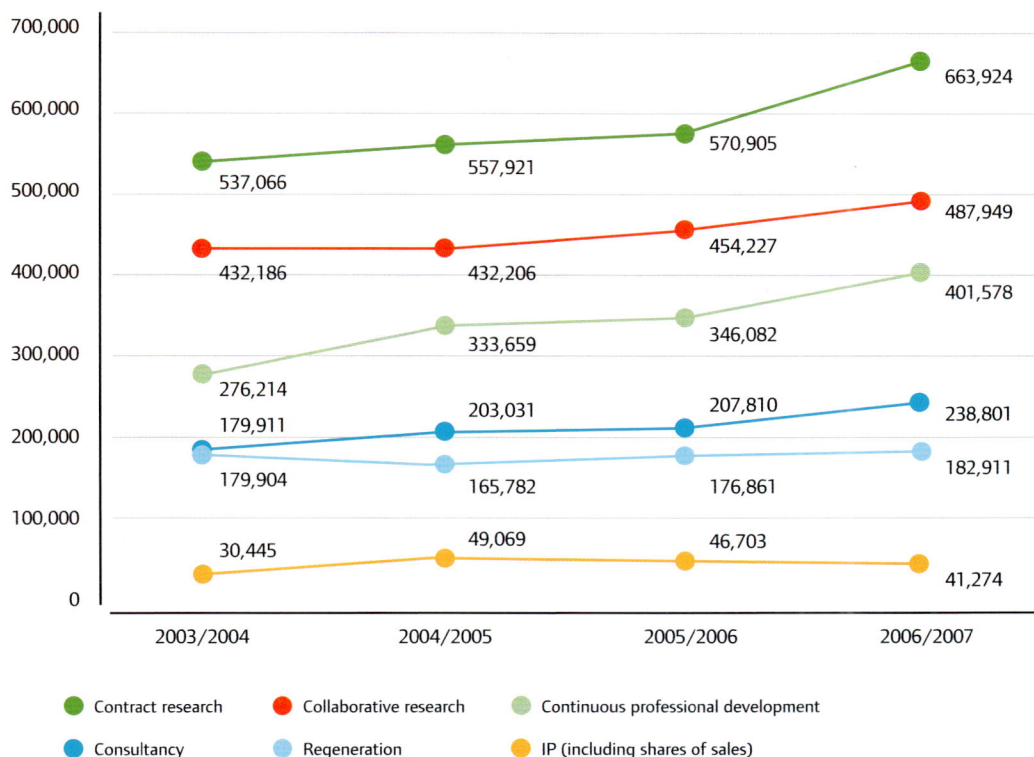

Legend:
- Contract research
- Collaborative research
- Continuous professional development
- Consultancy
- Regeneration
- IP (including shares of sales)

Data points:
- Contract research: 537,066 (2003/2004), 557,921 (2004/2005), 570,905 (2005/2006), 663,924 (2006/2007)
- Collaborative research: 432,186 (2003/2004), 432,206 (2004/2005), 454,227 (2005/2006), 487,949 (2006/2007)
- Continuous professional development: 276,214 (2003/2004), 333,659 (2004/2005), 346,082 (2005/2006), 401,578 (2006/2007)
- Consultancy: 179,911 (2003/2004), 203,031 (2004/2005), 207,810 (2005/2006), 238,801 (2006/2007)
- Regeneration: 179,904 (2003/2004), 165,782 (2004/2005), 176,861 (2005/2006), 182,911 (2006/2007)
- IP (including shares of sales): 30,445 (2003/2004), 49,069 (2004/2005), 46,703 (2005/2006), 41,274 (2006/2007)

Source: HEFCE, Higher Education – Business Community Interaction (HE-BCI) surveys 2003 – 2007.

of university-business interactions confirm the importance of multiple knowledge exchange mechanisms.[23] They highlight the importance of personal relationships, the development of trusting relationships between the partners and the importance of relational rather than contractual interactions. Based on this, it has been suggested that the differences between the intensity of interactions between universities and businesses in the UK and in the US may reflect differences in the absorptive capacity in UK firms, and by businesses' experience of working with universities and the ability to understand and relate to university academics. Variations in absorptive capacity can be explained by variations in management practices, training and the use of collaborative networks.[24] It seems fair to say that there is a limited understanding among researchers and practitioners of how to develop the 'connective capacity' between universities and business.

All this suggest that knowledge exchange works in a variety of ways, with informal knowledge transmission, consultancy and joint-research being important as well as the formal transfer of patents and licences.

4. Universities are also powerful network-builders

Universities have a powerful second-order effect in knowledge exchange between firms, by virtue of their role as anchors for clusters of innovative businesses. As our case studies demonstrate, often one of the biggest benefits for firms in setting up near a university is not the academic knowledge of the university itself, but of the presence of other firms attracted by the university. Universities can help facilitate this: consider the role of the University of Bath in hosting the Silicon South West organisation that supports the microelectronics industry around Bristol, Bath and Swindon. The role of universities in co-ordinating the development of industries can be seen in research by Cosh, Hughes and Lester, which showed the importance of universities not just in providing formal and informal knowledge, but also in acting as co-ordinators and providing 'public space' functions.[25]

Figure 2 highlights the importance not only of informal contacts with the university, but of the university's role in bringing people and

how innovative are we?' Cambridge, MA: MIT Institute, Centre for Business Research and Industrial Performance Centre.

Or from in-depth interviews and case studies of particular universities or departments. See Ham, R. and Mowery, D. (1998) Improving the effectiveness of public-private R&D collaboration: case studies at a US weapons laboratory. 'Research Policy.' 26, pp.661-675.

23. Abreu, M., Grinevich, V., Hughes, A., Kitson, M. and Ternouth, P. (2008) 'Universities Business Knowledge Exchange.' London and Cambridge: Council for Industry and Higher Education and Centre for Business Research.

24. Abreu, M., Grinevich, V., Kitson, M. and Savona, M. (2007) 'Absorptive Capacity and Regional Patterns of Innovation.' London: DIUS.

25. Cosh, A., Hughes, A. and Lester, R. (2006) 'UK PLC: Just how innovative are we?' Cambridge, MA: MIT Institute.

Figure 2: Types of university-business interaction contributing to innovation

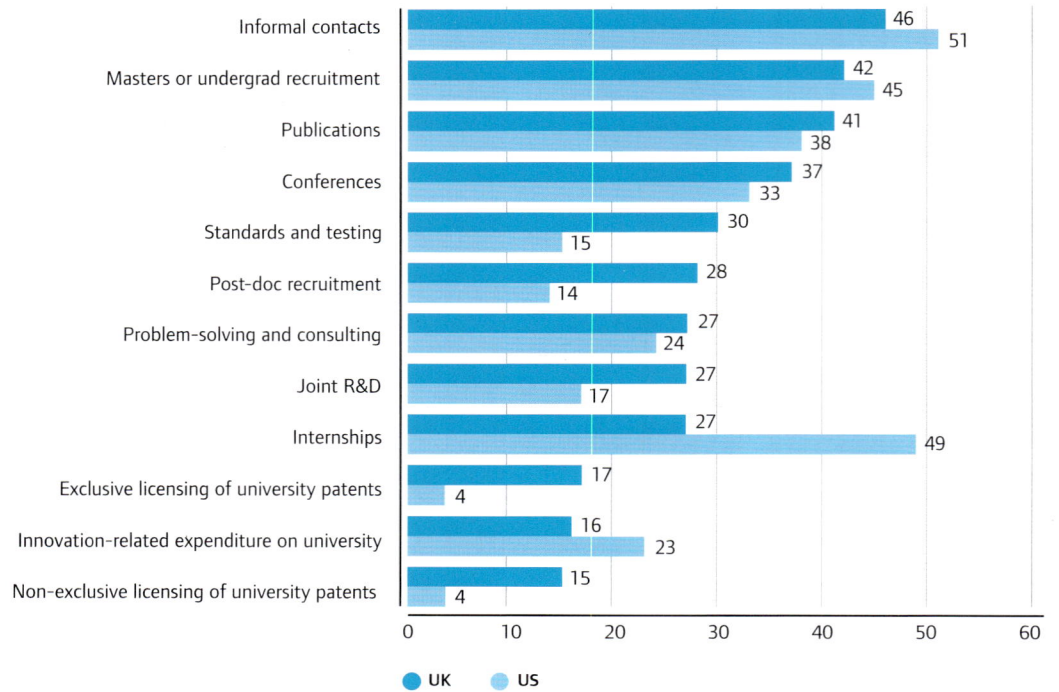

Type	UK	US
Informal contacts	46	51
Masters or undergrad recruitment	42	45
Publications	41	38
Conferences	37	33
Standards and testing	30	15
Post-doc recruitment	28	14
Problem-solving and consulting	27	24
Joint R&D	27	17
Internships	27	49
Exclusive licensing of university patents	17	4
Innovation-related expenditure on university	16	23
Non-exclusive licensing of university patents	15	4

● UK ● US

Source: Cosh, A., Hughes, A. and Lester, R. (2006) 'UK PLC: Just how innovative are we?' Cambridge M.A: MIT Institute.

Figure 3: Sources of information for innovation (Community Innovation Survey 2005 and 2007: percentage of respondents rating source as of some importance)

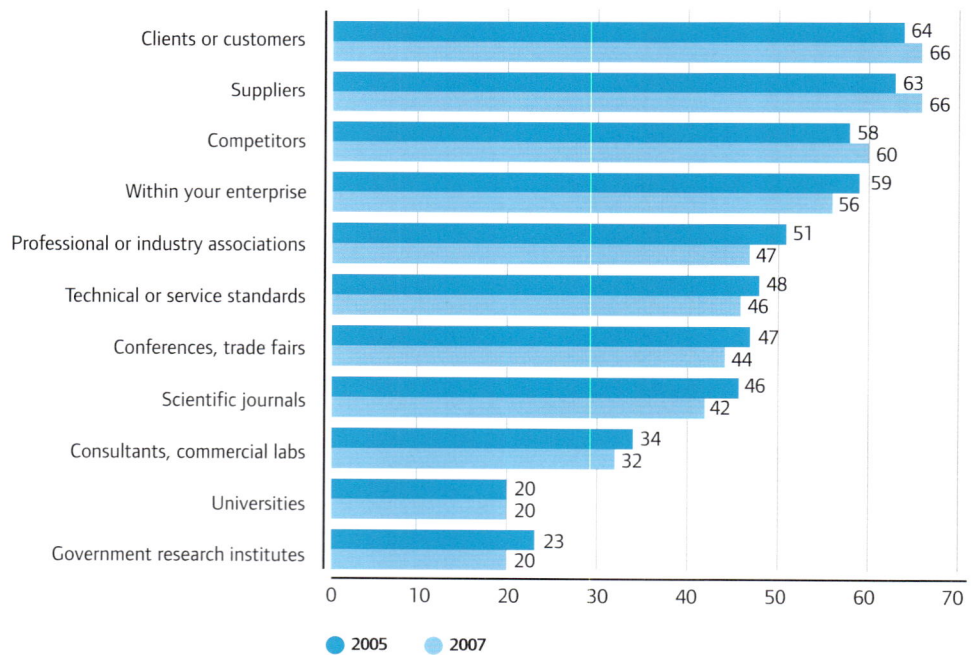

Source	2005	2007
Clients or customers	64	66
Suppliers	63	66
Competitors	58	60
Within your enterprise	59	56
Professional or industry associations	51	47
Technical or service standards	48	46
Conferences, trade fairs	47	44
Scientific journals	46	42
Consultants, commercial labs	34	32
Universities	20	20
Government research institutes	23	20

● 2005 ● 2007

Source: DIUS (2008) 'Persistence and change in UK innovation, 2002-06.' London: DIUS.

universities together, for example through organising conferences and standard-setting.

This is particularly important given the relative importance of other business in the corporate innovation process. Community Innovation Survey data have repeatedly shown that businesses on average regard other businesses as more important sources of innovation than universities (see Figure 3).

The economic role of universities varies according to the nature of local economies
The role of universities in the regional innovation process depends on the local economic structure and on the strengths of the university in question. Richard Lester, the MIT industrial innovation specialist, has argued that there are four types of local economic evolution that can be influenced by university-business interactions:[26]

- New industry formation: developing entirely new sectors, often based on novel technologies and university research.

- Industry transplantation: bringing existing (but often higher value) industries to a region.

- Diversification into technologically-related industries: for example, in helping 'phoenix industries' to develop from declining firms.

- Upgrading of existing industries: providing technical problem-solving advice and skills development for existing businesses.

As shown in Table 2, these different pathways will require different types and combinations of university-business interactions. It is important to note that each type of local economic evolution requires a variety of types of support

26. Lester, R. (2005) 'Universities, Innovation, and the Competitiveness of Local Economies: A Summary Report from the Local Innovation Systems Project — Phase I.' MIT Industrial Performance Center Working Paper 05-010. Cambridge, MA: MIT.

Table 2: University roles in alternative regional innovation-led growth pathways

Type of economic development	University roles
New industry formation	Forefront science and engineering research
	Aggressive technology licensing policies
	Promote/assist entrepreneurial business (incubation services, etc.)
	Cultivate ties between academic researchers and local entrepreneurs
	Create an industry identity: standard setting, evangelists, convening conferences, workshops and entrepreneurs forums etc.
Industry transplantation	Education/manpower development
	Responsive curricula
	Technical assistance for sub-contractors, suppliers
Diversification into technologically-related industries	Bridging between disconnected actors
	Filling 'structural holes'
	Creating an industry identity
Upgrading of existing industries	Problem-solving for industry through contract research, faculty consulting, etc.
	Education/manpower development
	Global best practice
	Convening foresight exercises
	Convening user-supplier forums

Source: Lester, R. K. (2005) 'Universities, Innovation, and the Competitiveness of Local Economies: A Summary Report from the Local Innovation Systems Project— Phase I.' Cambridge, MA: MIT Industrial Performance Center Working Paper 05-010.

from universities. New industry formation requires not only formal knowledge transfer (Lester's 'forefront science and engineering research' and 'aggressive technology licensing policies'), but also network-building ('creating an industry identity') and informal knowledge exchange ('cultivating ties between academic researchers and local entrepreneurs').

In the UK, there has been a focus on the creation of new industries such as the formation of high-tech clusters in knowledge-generating sectors such as ICT, biotechnology and, more recently, cleantech. There has been less focus on the wider knowledge exchange mechanisms through which universities can contribute to regional economic development particularly in the areas of enabling the development of an industry that is new to the region; the diversification into technologically-related industries and the upgrading of existing industries.

Part 2: Case Studies

The Cambridge Phenomenon: A high-tech cluster with the university at its heart

The world-class biotechnology and information technology cluster around the University of Cambridge is frequently cited as an example of the impact that a university can have on its local economy and how it can support regional development. The cluster would probably have not existed without the presence of the university and the draw of its strong research base and a supply of skilled recruitment. However, the emergence of the Cambridge high-tech cluster with a strong university at its heart was not intended nor strategically planned.

The university generates significant economic impact

The University of Cambridge is one of the world's leading universities and an economic actor in its own right. It employs more than 11,700 people directly and indirectly supports more than 77,000 jobs in the Eastern region of the UK. If the University did not exist, the economic impact on the UK economy over the next ten years would be a £4.4 billion loss in GDP and approximately 10,800 fewer jobs, and the impact on the region would be even greater, "requiring replacement of a net present value of £21.2 billion in GDP and approximately 77,000 jobs".[27]

Organic growth of university collaboration

A snapshot of the Cambridge economy today shows many thriving high-tech businesses, particularly in the area of biotechnology, combined with a host of university departments and organisations whose role is to promote industry collaboration.[28] In 2006/07 the university generated over £49 million in income, just under £3.5 million of this from IP. It filed 112 patents and 35 licences, creating two spin-outs, with a total of 45 active spin-outs.[29] Although many high-tech businesses that locate in Cambridge do not have direct connections with the university, some have very strong links and have established embedded laboratories, where teams of scientists co-locate and collaborate with academics or an academic department. For example, Hitachi, Toshiba, Pfizer and Microsoft all have high-quality facilities in Cambridge. However, their arrival is relatively recent and reflects the serendipitous and non-prescribed growth of the Cambridge cluster.

Such a snapshot does not indicate the dynamics of growth of the Cambridge cluster, which initially developed when the university took little active interest in business engagement. It is indicative that in 2009 the university celebrates its 800th anniversary, but its Business School only celebrates its 20th anniversary.

The origins of the cluster – a perfect storm

The university has a long tradition of scientific research[30] and the city has been home to high-tech businesses for over a hundred years. But the start of the phenomenon can be traced to the 1970s, which saw a growth of firms specialising in information technology especially computer-aided design. The university adopted a laissez-faire approach, in that staff contracts did not prescribe what an academic could or should do and there was a relaxed view on intellectual property rights.[31] Some academics embarked on technological commercialisation, most did not. Another important factor was the availability of finance, as Barclays Bank (in particular the local manager, Walter Herriot) took an enlightened,

27. Library House (2006) 'Cambridge Cluster Report 2006.' Cambridge: Library House.

28. The Judge Business School; the Institute for Manufacturing whose research and education programmes are underpinned by close engagement with industry; the Cambridge Programme for Sustainability Leadership which works with business, public sector and civil society leaders on issues such as climate change, resource depletion and poverty; Cambridge Enterprise which helps academics make their ideas and concepts more commercially successful; and a Research Services Division which manages funding from external organisations.

29. HEFCE (2008) 'Higher education-business and community interaction survey: 2006–07.' Available at: http://www.hefce.ac.uk/pubs/hefce/2008/08_22/

30. Including the work of Newton and Darwin, Crick and Watson, Babbage and Hawking.

31. SQW (1985) 'The Cambridge Phenomenon: The Growth of High Technology in a University Town.' Cambridge: SQW; SQW (2000) 'The Cambridge Phenomenon Revisited.' Vols 1 and 2. Cambridge: SQW.

and at that time unusual, view to providing start-up finance and advice for high-tech firms.

The Cambridge phenomenon emerged from a 'perfect storm' of entrepreneurial scientists, enlightened finance and a laissez-faire attitude from the university, a mixture of serendipity and luck. This suggests that it is a phenomenon that cannot be easily replicated elsewhere. It is no accident that this unplanned approach did not result in other universities developing high-tech clusters in the 1970s and 1980s.

The development of the cluster – changing dynamics and new challenges

As the cluster has grown its dynamics have changed, and it has now reached critical mass where the key factors are the availability of skilled labour and finance. An important local driver is the labour market, as highly skilled workers are more willing to work for a Cambridge-based enterprise than one located elsewhere. Working in a high-tech enterprise is often associated with unstable employment, as many firms fail. This problem can be mitigated by the prospect of being re-employed in the same local labour market – a prospect which is made more likely by the large number of firms engaged in similar activities.[32]

Another important local driver is the access to finance. A Cambridge location often signals credibility to the mainly London-based venture capitalists and the expansion of the cluster has led to the development of local intermediaries and support institutions including locally-based venture capital.

Supporting the high-tech cluster as an engine of economic recovery

If both the university and the cluster did not exist then the total economic impact for the UK would mean the "the need to find up to a net present value of £57.5 billion in replacement GDP and 154,000 new jobs".[33] Recessionary challenges make the further development of the cluster more pressing. There has been particular growth in biotechnology firms and more recently cleantech businesses. Collaborative R&D links have been fostered between the university ('eds') and Addenbrokes, the local teaching hospital ('meds') to accelerate drug production, in the hope that this will act as a powerful local economic engine.[34] Supporting growth in this sector is strategically important for the university, regional and national economy.

32. Kitson, M. and Primost, D. (2005) 'Corporate Responses to Macroeconomic Changes and Shocks.' End of Award Report. Swindon: ESRC.
33. Library House (2006) 'Cambridge Cluster Report 2006.' Cambridge: Library House. p.10.
34. Harkavy, I. and Zuckerman, H. (1999) 'Eds and Meds: Cities' Hidden Assets.' Washington, DC: The Brookings Institution.

A Cambridge spin-out: Light Blue Optics[35]

Light Blue Optics (LBO) formed in January 2004 as a spin-out from the University of Cambridge Engineering Department, developing miniature projection systems. As a spin-out the university holds a small equity stake. The company's holographic laser projection technology delivers full colour, high-quality video images that remain in focus at all distances. The technology's efficiency and small size make it suitable for applications across a range of markets. In October 2007, LBO closed a $26 million Series 'A' funding round, led by Earlybird Venture Capital and Capital-E. Existing investors – 3i, who led LBO's $3.5 million seed-funding round in 2006, and NESTA – also participated. The money will enable LBO to accelerate its product development and commercialisation programme towards the high-volume manufacture of miniature projection systems. LBO estimates that the total available market for miniature projection systems will exceed $5 billion by 2012. Dr Adrian Cable, one of LBO's founders and the current Chief Technology Officer, is a Cambridge graduate with a PhD in holographic optics. The other three founders are also Cambridge PhD graduates and remain with the company.

Spin out success at the University of Southampton

The University of Southampton has enjoyed disproportionate success in creating spin-outs from its research. Since 1969, the university has launched over 50 spin-out companies in fields such as oil and gas exploration, pharmaceuticals and nanotechnology. The University has collaborated with a wide range of business partners, such as QinetiQ, IBM, Microsoft, Rolls Royce and BAE Systems.

The University of Southampton is ranked third in the world for creating spin-outs, behind only Stanford and Cambridge.[36] This is despite being placed over 150 positions below Stanford and Cambridge in the Shanghai Jiao Tong University Ranking system.[37] This suggests that the university has a particularly effective approach that facilitates technology transfer, knowledge exchange and the creation of spin-outs.

Since 2000 there have been 12 successful spin-outs. Three of these have floated on the Alternative Investment Market with a combined market capitalisation value of £160 million.[38] The university has generated income through disposal of some of its shareholdings at float, and two of these companies remain in the region, including SPI Lasers, which was sold to German company Trumpf in 2008 for £28 million.

Structured serendipity

In the past, the university focused on a 'push' model of technology transfer, with academia supplying ideas, R&D, technical support and technological innovations for companies to commercialise. This university recognised some challenges in this model: it requires brokerage to the demand side, which was more obviously the domain of professional and specialist business services with experience of technological commercialisation, sourcing investment and taking products to market.

University management put in place structures that reflect and respond to this barrier. Southampton provides a range of business support services based on an ethos of 'structured serendipity'. This means that rather than a prescriptive pipeline of activity, Southampton offers consultancy services, knowledge exchange schemes and business incubation designed to support any and all types of commercialisation opportunity, delivered through the right mix of academic and industry-skilled people. The University of Southampton is the one of UK's top ranked

institutions for collaboration with small and medium-sized companies.[39]

Consultancy services and knowledge exchange schemes

There are seven consultancy units with 125 staff that generate £7.5 million revenue per annum. They provide business support and help to secure public and private research grants, which accounts for 40 per cent of Southampton research, in areas such as nanotechnology, stem cell research and alternate fuel development. The Knowledge Transfer Partnership portfolio is worth over £1.7 million. One example is Shell STEP (Shell Technology Enterprise Programme), which in 2008 placed over 600 students in Hampshire-based small and medium-sized companies.

Business incubation with SETsquared

The ability of Southampton to incubate and spin out promising companies is supported by the SETsquared Partnership, an entrepreneurial collaboration between the Universities of Bath, Bristol, Southampton and Surrey. The campus Business Incubation Centre supports the growth of early-stage high-tech companies with access to a network of experienced entrepreneurs, academics, potential investors, investment advisers and business professionals. In the last four years, SETsquared companies have raised over £120 million investment and created more than 1,000 new jobs.[40]

International collaboration

The university has built up a strong relationship with the University of California, San Diego and the University of California, Irvine, as a result of the Science Bridges initiative. The universities collaborate in research projects, and exchange knowledge and best practice in building entrepreneurial skills, the commercial development of technology and expertise in spin-outs. Successful US-UK collaboration has encouraged UK policy to widen the scope of this initiative to China and India.[41] Southampton has built up its own links with China and Thailand to promote collaboration and access to new markets for local companies.

Attacking the recession in Southampton: growth in the emerging green economy

As the recession deepens and the UK seeks out new areas of growth, South Hampshire is well placed to build on regional strength in the expanding cleantech sector. Ilika, as described overleaf, is one of six South Hampshire companies working in energy and cleantech, three of which are university spin-outs. This is more than any other European location except

35. See http://www.nesta.org.uk/light-blue-optics/

36. Library House (2007) 'An Analysis of UK University Technology and Knowledge Transfer Activities.' Cambridge: Library House.

37. See http://www.arwu.org/rank2008/Top500_EN(by%20rank).pdf

38. See http://www.soton.ac.uk/about/economic_impact/index.shtml

39. HEFCE (2008) 'Higher education-business and community interaction survey: 2006–07.' Available at: http://www.hefce.ac.uk/pubs/hefce/2008/08_22/

40. See http://www.setsquaredpartnership.co.uk/news-events/news/?n=327

41. RCUK press release (2 February 2009) 'RCUK Science Bridges Awards announced.' Available at: http://www.rcuk.ac.uk/news/090130.htm

London, and has been recognised as a hotspot by the 2008 Guardian/Library House CleanTech 100.[42]

The UK is already a major player in the £3 trillion global market for low carbon goods and services. The UK low carbon and environmental sector is worth £107 billion a year. In 2007, the UK attracted 30 per cent of all European venture capital investment in cleantech.[43] The drive for a green economy is forecast to produce 7 per cent growth per year (2008 to 2013).[44]

To support the crucial growth of this sector, the government must ensure an adequate supply of funding and policy support for South Hampshire's infrastructure, its facilities for research and development and the skills of its workers to make it an obvious international destination for low carbon industry. Given Southampton's successful track record in spinning out commercial ventures, this would seem an area of strategic importance.

A better planning system and transport infrastructure
The Vice-Chancellor has actively driven a programme of collaboration between the university, the city and the regional economy through informal and formal economic partnerships. While this has supported regional economic development, it has yet to resolve some framework policy issues that could deter future growth.

Planning regulations on the University of Southampton's Science Park have blocked private companies from coming on-site. Two healthcare clinics were recently turned away because they did not fit the research or manufacturing criteria, despite their obvious benefits. It is important that this type of barrier does not prevent building up South Hampshire and Southampton as a leader in cleantech and other sectors, or its ability to attract investment.

As a coast location Southampton only has 180° exposure. A lack of a fully integrated and well-linked transport infrastructure would deter companies from locating in the region, especially foreign investors. This is an area where co-operation between the university and South Hampshire authorities will be important for local economic success.

42. See http://www.guardian. co.uk/environment/ table/2008/sep/18/ cleantech100fulllist. cleantechnology100

43. BERR (2009) Low Carbon Industrial Strategy: A vision.' London: BERR. Available at: http://www.berr.gov.uk/ files/file50373.pdf

44. NESTA (2009) 'Demanding Growth: Why the UK needs a recovery plan based on growth and innovation.' London: NESTA. Available at: http://www.nesta. org.uk/assets/Uploads/ pdf/Research-Report/ demanding_growth_report_ NESTA.pdf

A Southampton spin-out: Ilika

Ilika Technologies Ltd spun out from Southampton's Chemistry Department in 2004. It has established itself as a profitable and innovative growth company in the field of materials development, for example creating better batteries and fuel cells. The development of novel materials makes the company of interest to a number of large sectors, such as energy, automotive, electronics and biomedical. This success has helped to secure three rounds of funding, with the latest round of £7 million completed in August 2007. There is a diverse set of international shareholders, in part a reflection of the wide market appeal of the company. The CEO believes that the business support services from the university and SETsquared facilitated the spin-out process. Easy access to a range of professionals and an agreed IP framework allowed the company to focus on securing investment for growth. The company retains strong ties with the university, as a source of knowledge and recruitment.

The University of Newcastle: developing networks between business and academia

Regenerating Newcastle and the North East
The University of Newcastle has a strong track record of providing research-based advice to local industries. In recent years, it has undertaken work to deepen its relationship with local businesses by investing in individuals who can bridge the gap between academia, the research base and industry, in particular its Professors of Practice programme.

After decades of decline in Newcastle's shipbuilding industry, a variety of regional partners have focused on rehabilitating the region's economic and social standing. Their primary objectives are to increase regional GVA to 90 per cent of the national average (from 79 per cent in 2007) and to create 22,000 new businesses.[45] A central element of this approach is to capitalise on pockets of scientific excellence in order to improve the region's competitive position, and initiate and sustain a regeneration process driven by research, development and innovation.

Investing in the science and research base through Newcastle Science City
Investment has, in part, been intended to stimulate activities that facilitate the commercial exploitation of scientific research, ensuring that specialist business support services are available to scientists, science and technology entrepreneurs, start-ups and businesses.

To help meet economic challenges, in 2004 the government designated Newcastle as one of six English Science Cities, intended to develop closer links between the science and technology research base and industry, in order to facilitate commercial activity and growth. In partnership, the City Council, One NorthEast and the university guide the direction of the Science City.

A central regional role for the university
The University of Newcastle has performed well in traditional measures of technology transfer. In 2006/07 it received just under £16 million income from collaboration. It received £370,000 in income from IP, filed 44 patents and generated four licences. There are 11 active spin-outs associated with the university.[46] However, these activities only go part of the way to achieving the university's economic ambitions. Even with the Science City there remains a crucial gap in linking

the demands of industry and the supply from the research base. Newcastle decided it needed to invest in other ways of increasing university-business collaboration, specifically by developing a group of 'boundary spanners'; people with academic and industry experience and understanding, with access to networks on both sides of the interaction. The Professors of Practice initiative is designed to create such a bridging role.

Boundary-spanning Professors of Practice
The Professors of Practice (POPs) programme was established in 2004. POPs are individuals intended to integrate and align the interest of the university and industry, identifying and making the most of potential common interests.

POPs have been appointed by the Business School in three strategic areas: Ageing & Health, Biomolecular Engineering and Drug Discovery. Their remit is to provide leadership and work closely with the scientists, Business School faculty and Newcastle Science City in order to promote commercialisation opportunities for the university in these strategic areas. This includes the promotion of industrial networks, developing translational research programmes, identifying commercialisation opportunities and acting as a role model for staff and students through their teaching and coaching activities.

Professors of Practice are typically scientist-entrepreneurs who are currently running their own business or otherwise engaged in senior management positions. In order to fulfil this role, they maintain their dual affiliation with businesses and the university on a part-time contractual basis (this is part of a broader trend: in the US, by 2001, non-tenure track faculty members were about 34 per cent of the total full-time academics).

POPs support collaboration initiatives, organise university-business events, are innovation role models and support future regional growth targets
Professors of Practice have conducted a range of activities that demonstrate an impact in building university-business relations.

POPs have been involved in supporting the planning of the University Research Centre in Biopharmaceutical and Bioprocessing Technology Centre (BBTC) by capitalising on research expertise of the School of Chemical Engineering and Advanced Materials and engaging with industrial partners. The venture

45. One North East (2008) 'Corporate Plan 2008-13.' Newcastle Upon Tyne: One North East.
46. HEFCE (2008) 'Higher education-business and community interaction survey: 2006–07.' Available at: http://www.hefce.ac.uk/pubs/hefce/2008/08_22/

has been successful in securing £20 million funding from the EPSRC for an Engineering Doctorate and Training Programme in Bioprocess Technologies. They have also helped secure funding for a dedicated Director of Industrial Liaison for the BBTC.

They have co-ordinated university-business events that promote knowledge exchange and facilitate collaboration opportunities, such as 'Conversaziones in BioBusiness'. POPs have also secured an international conference on Ageing and Health in 2010 expecting to attract 500 delegates.

A third role is that of embodiment of the vision set out by Newcastle Science City to promote innovation. Under this remit, POPs are acting as innovation role models, by participating in the Regional Innovation Awards, representing Newcastle Science City at the National Science City Summit and the Regional Universities Blue Print business planning competition.

Finally, they can support future regional growth plans. Newcastle Science City is now being taken forward as a company limited by guarantee. Newcastle University, Newcastle City Council and One NorthEast have each invested £1.37 million over the next three years and in return the company has the target of creating 30 companies and supporting 183 companies. POPs can play an important role in developing the university-business collaborations that can help meet these targets and support regional growth.

Who is a POP?

Professor Peter Gore is an expert in Ageing and Health. He has over 25 years experience in medical product design and set up the company ADL Smartcare to match people with technology-based solutions. Peter works with the University's Institute for Ageing and Health and is helping to plan a Campus for Ageing and Vitality, for example helping to secure funding and external partners, such as Tesco.

The University of Manchester: translating medical research into practice

The University of Manchester has a strong record in the production of health research and the subsequent commercialisation of products and services. It has recently embarked on a series of major institutional projects to build wide-ranging links with clinicians, pharmaceutical firms and medical device makers to improve the contribution it makes to the economy. These are the Biomedical Research Centre, a Centre for Integrating Medicine and Innovative Technology, and an Academic Health Centre, which have the potential to drive up business innovation from the medical research base, notably in biotechnology, contributing to regional growth.

The North West of England has a heritage in the sector, dating back to the development of the chemicals industry in the late 18th century, which in turn led to pharmaceuticals. Indeed, Liverpool was one of the first sites to manufacture penicillin by fermentation during World War II. Figure 4 shows cluster development in North West England from 1700 onwards.

University-business collaboration in biotechnology

Manchester, and the North West region more generally, are home to a growing biomedical cluster underpinned by a major pharmaceutical presence, a rapidly expanding biotechnology community, and internationally renowned academic and clinical research strengths. Figure 5 shows the biomedical cluster in the North West of England today. The region now houses around 200 biomedical companies including firms such as DxS and Myconostica, major health-related companies such as SSL and Unilever, and branches of seven multinational pharmaceutical firms, including AstraZeneca and GlaxoSmithKline. The sector employs 20,000 people and the region is the highest exporter of pharmaceuticals in the UK; in 2003 exports were £3.4 billion.[47]

The University of Manchester performs well in technology transfer, under the guidance of The University of Manchester Intellectual Property Ltd (UMIP). In 2006/07 the university generated over £30 million in collaborative income, and £5 million of income from IP. The university filed 38 patents, generated seven spin-outs and had 42 active spin-outs.[48]

The development of the biomedical sector is recognised by the North West Development Agency (NWDA) as a priority for the Manchester city-region, and a source of productivity and growth. The University of Manchester has been developing new organisational infrastructure designed to expand healthcare innovation and so support the regions offer and commercial attraction.

Three recent biomedical initiatives involving the university

The Manchester Biomedical Research Centre (2008) is a £35 million partnership of the Central Manchester & Manchester Children's University Hospitals NHS Trust and the University of Manchester, funded by the National Institute for Health Research. The Centre is focused on translational research, with projects aimed at tackling some of the highest priority disease areas of the Manchester population. The Centre will receive additional funding from the NWDA, Manchester City Council and its commercial partners include AstraZeneca and GlaxoSmithKline. The GVA impacts of this initiative are estimated to be £111 million at the local level and £127 million at a regional level and over 100 new jobs will be created in the city over the next three years.

Manchester: Integrating Medicine and Innovative Technology (MIMIT, 2008) supports translational research by multidisciplinary teams for medical device and clinical technology system applications. It supports knowledge creation, exchange and new product development in Manchester. MIMIT brings together the university with the city-region's five major teaching hospitals to explore demand-based technological R&D. MIMIT provides seed funding (competitively awarded by a Scientific Committee) and currently supports nine projects. MIMIT has recently won a £1.3 million Science Bridges award from the EPSRC to further its development.

The *Manchester Academic Health Science Centre* (2008) brings together Manchester's existing research activity and research partnerships from six NHS organisations and The University of Manchester. The Centre aims to combine excellence in academia, clinical service delivery, research management and education to help create and exploit new biomedical opportunities. With over £100 million a year currently invested in health research in the Greater Manchester area, it is believed that co-ordinating and channelling clinical and academic research strengths under one umbrella will help to secure more

47. North West Science (2007) 'North West Science Strategy 2007–2010.' Warrington: North West Science. Available at: http://www.northwestscience.co.uk/uploads/documents/apr_07/northwestscience_1176911562_Science_Strat_07.pdf

48. HEFCE (2008) 'Higher education–business and community interaction survey: 2006–07.' Available at: http://www.hefce.ac.uk/pubs/hefce/2008/08_22/

investment from industry, government and charitable bodies as well as generate health benefits and economic development in Manchester and the wider North West.

Attacking the recession in Manchester and the North West: supporting growth in the biomedical cluster

Companies which have emerged from the university have attracted over £150 million of funding over the last five years and include successes such as Renovo, fast becoming a world leader in drugs to improve the appearance of scars and enhance wound healing, listed on the London Stock Exchange and valued at approximately £300 million.[49] Companies like Ai2, F2G and Muscagen are developing innovative products and services in the biomedical sector.[50]

In 2008 UMIP teamed up with one of the UK's leading technology investment managers, MTI, to create a vehicle for providing academics with access to capital to develop world-leading research and exploit opportunities for technological commercialisation. The Fund will have preferred access to all investment opportunities generated. The Fund raised initial backing of €42 million (£32 million) from a range of investors, making it Europe's largest institutional fund to have a single university focus. It makes investments of £250,000 to £750,000 in young technology companies, with follow-on funding possible.[51] The biomedical sector has a large domestic market as well as international appeal and is a promising growth area.

49. See http://www.nesta.org.uk/spin-out-venture-fund-achieves-first-close/

50. Ai2 develops innovative technology to prevent infection on a wide range of commonly used medical devices like urinary catheters, stents and wound dressings; F2G develops novel agents to treat serious fungal disease; Muscagen Ltd, a joint University of Cardiff/University of Manchester spinout (based in Cardiff) develops selective compounds for therapeutic use in treatments covering disorders such as dementia, incontinence and cardiovascular disease.

51. See http://www.nesta.org.uk/spin-out-venture-fund-achieves-first-close/

Figure 4: Cluster evolution in North West England: 1700 onwards

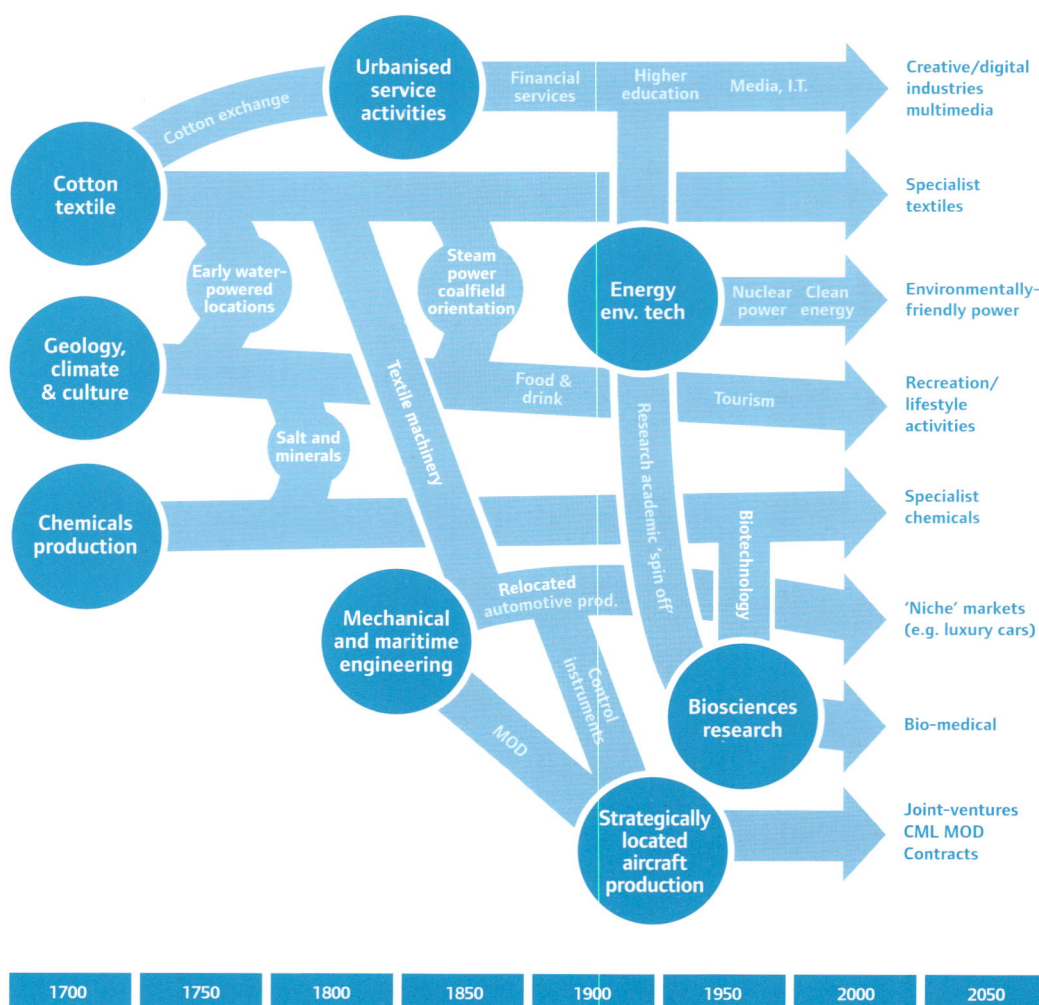

Source: Oakey, R (2003) 'North West clusters: a timeline evolution study.' Manchester: Manchester Business School, University of Manchester.

Figure 5: The biomedical cluster in the North West of England today

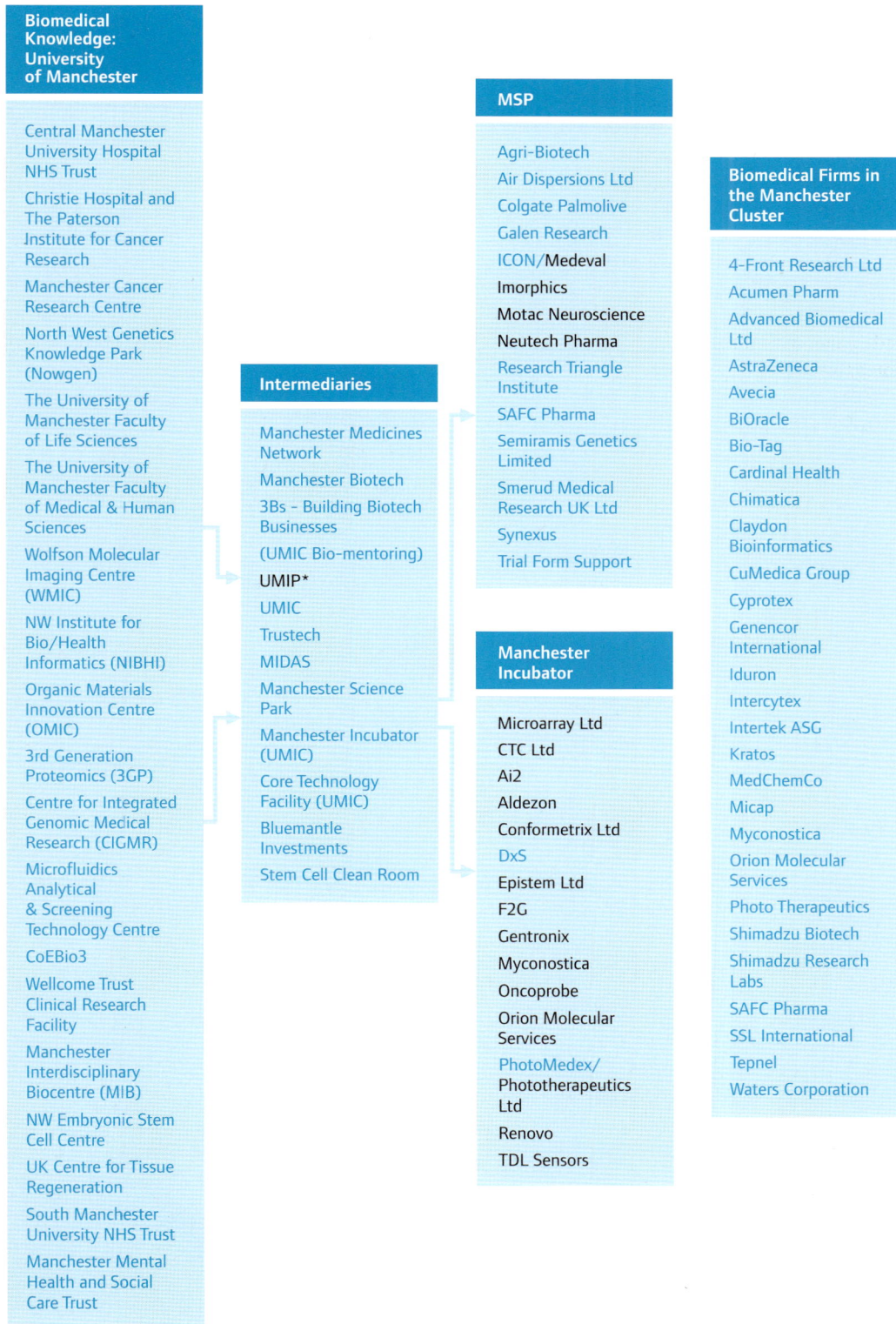

Biomedical Knowledge: University of Manchester

- Central Manchester University Hospital NHS Trust
- Christie Hospital and The Paterson Institute for Cancer Research
- Manchester Cancer Research Centre
- North West Genetics Knowledge Park (Nowgen)
- The University of Manchester Faculty of Life Sciences
- The University of Manchester Faculty of Medical & Human Sciences
- Wolfson Molecular Imaging Centre (WMIC)
- NW Institute for Bio/Health Informatics (NIBHI)
- Organic Materials Innovation Centre (OMIC)
- 3rd Generation Proteomics (3GP)
- Centre for Integrated Genomic Medical Research (CIGMR)
- Microfluidics Analytical & Screening Technology Centre
- CoEBio3
- Wellcome Trust Clinical Research Facility
- Manchester Interdisciplinary Biocentre (MIB)
- NW Embryonic Stem Cell Centre
- UK Centre for Tissue Regeneration
- South Manchester University NHS Trust
- Manchester Mental Health and Social Care Trust

Intermediaries

- Manchester Medicines Network
- Manchester Biotech
- 3Bs - Building Biotech Businesses
- (UMIC Bio-mentoring)
- UMIP*
- UMIC
- Trustech
- MIDAS
- Manchester Science Park
- Manchester Incubator (UMIC)
- Core Technology Facility (UMIC)
- Bluemantle Investments
- Stem Cell Clean Room

MSP

- Agri-Biotech
- Air Dispersions Ltd
- Colgate Palmolive
- Galen Research
- ICON/Medeval
- Imorphics
- Motac Neuroscience
- Neutech Pharma
- Research Triangle Institute
- SAFC Pharma
- Semiramis Genetics Limited
- Smerud Medical Research UK Ltd
- Synexus
- Trial Form Support

Manchester Incubator

- Microarray Ltd
- CTC Ltd
- Ai2
- Aldezon
- Conformetrix Ltd
- DxS
- Epistem Ltd
- F2G
- Gentronix
- Myconostica
- Oncoprobe
- Orion Molecular Services
- PhotoMedex/ Phototherapeutics Ltd
- Renovo
- TDL Sensors

Biomedical Firms in the Manchester Cluster

- 4-Front Research Ltd
- Acumen Pharm
- Advanced Biomedical Ltd
- AstraZeneca
- Avecia
- BiOracle
- Bio-Tag
- Cardinal Health
- Chimatica
- Claydon Bioinformatics
- CuMedica Group
- Cyprotex
- Genencor International
- Iduron
- Intercytex
- Intertek ASG
- Kratos
- MedChemCo
- Micap
- Myconostica
- Orion Molecular Services
- Photo Therapeutics
- Shimadzu Biotech
- Shimadzu Research Labs
- SAFC Pharma
- SSL International
- Tepnel
- Waters Corporation

* Black text dentotes Manchester spin-out

Source: UMIP (2006) 'Manchester Bio Community' University of Manchester Incubator Company.

The microelectronics industry in the South West

The thriving semiconductor cluster that has emerged in the Bristol-Swindon corridor and beyond owes much to the efforts of local universities. Universities have contributed not only intellectual property and spin-outs, but also a host of skilled employees, informal 'boundary-spanning' knowledge and cluster support skills. The result has been a wealth of start-ups, and a number of high-profile 'spin-ins' – semiconductor firms choosing to locate in the area because of the attraction of the cluster.

There has been a long tradition of innovation in the Bristol area – going back to Brunel, Concorde and, more recently, Wallace and Gromit (produced by Bristol-based Aardman Animations). The area is now home to the UK's largest concentration of silicon designers, double the size of that in Cambridge, the closest domestic competitor, and second only to the USA. Currently, the cluster consists of around 50 companies that directly employ approximately 5,000 people. Figure 6 shows a map of the firms across the region. A supportive ecosystem and infrastructure, in particular support from the Universities of Bristol and Bath, combined with a highly skilled workforce that the universities have helped create and attract, has fostered an active start-up culture. Figure 7 shows that in the last decade, start-ups in the South West have attracted more than $550 million in investment and have returned more than $800 million to shareholders.

Cluster development – a skilled labour pool
The origins of the cluster can be traced to the development of the specialist skills base in the local labour market. This skills pool developed at Inmos in Bristol and GEC-Plessey Semiconductor in Swindon in the 1980s, trained a generation of silicon designers. Although these companies have changed radically they have left a legacy of local skills that has helped to transform the local economy – they have been an important input into innovations in microprocessors, telecommunications and networking system design.

The knowledge base and knowledge exchange
The Bristol city-region has four major universities: Bath Spa University, and the Universities of Bath, Bristol and the West of England. There are many areas of research strength including digital technologies (especially in relation to computing and the creative and sector), advanced engineering (including aerospace), environmental technologies, and medical technologies and life sciences. A range of knowledge exchange mechanisms are being used in the Bristol city-region.

Bristol was made one of the UK's science cities in November 2005 to help the development of stronger links between business and the science base and ensure that innovation succeeded in becoming the engine of local economic growth. SETsquared, as described in more detail in the Southampton case study, actively supports business incubation through the co-ordinated range of support services it offers. Silicon South West provides support and networking opportunities for start-up and early-stage companies through its network of 1,300 members. Established four years ago, it is managed by the University of Bath's technology transfer office (Bath Ventures), is funded through industry sponsorship and also collaborates with SETsquared. Links between the microelectronics sector and the regions' universities also exist at a faculty level. Notably, David May, the lead architect of Inmos' transputer and the current Chief Technology Officer of the semiconductor firm XMOS, has been a professor at Bristol since 1995 and has in that time played a fundamental, boundary-spanning role in developing the sector.

Knowledge Transfer Partnerships (KTPs) have provided expertise to regional companies who wish to innovate or expand, notably SMEs. There are 20 KTPs in the Bristol city-region, helping to connect local companies to the knowledge base. In 2004, the four universities in the city-region combined with the University of Gloucestershire, the Royal Agricultural College and Business Link to form 'Knowledge West'. This consortium brings business and higher education communities together through collaborative initiatives, networks, events and a continuing professional development programme, producing qualitative impacts that support knowledge exchange, such as increasing university links to business and the development of companies.[52] Even though this HEIF-funded project will end soon, many of the schemes will carry on and continue to benefit the region.

Attractor of global business and 'spin-ins'
The cluster has helped to attract high levels of inward investment from large multinationals such as Orange, Toshiba, HP Labs, Motorola,

52. Forthcoming Evaluation of Knowledge West Project, Summer 2009.

Panasonic and ST Microelectronics – all have corporate R&D sites based in the region. Other international electronics companies such as Intel and Broadcom have a significant presence in the region, while semiconductor design companies such as Wolfson and Dialog Semiconductors have set up design centres in the South West in order to tap into the local skills. Companies spun-in have been attracted by the knowledge base as well as skills offer, including Systems4Silicon, Sidonis, Power Oasis and Xintronix. Silicon South West also supports links with international partners, marketing the region as widely as America, France, Taiwan, Japan and Israel.

Supporting and expanding the Silicon South West

Innovation, knowledge exchange and recruitment from the local universities, building on local strengths, have helped build the diversity of the region and increase economic growth – both by encouraging new firm formation and by acting as an attractor of major international companies.

This case study demonstrates the impact and importance of developing synergies between the university research and skills base, associated business support mechanisms and large and small firms. It demonstrates good practice in knowledge exchange and business innovation, and the non-academic role a university can play in the regional ecosystem.

Gnodal

Founded in 2008, Gnodal develops innovative networking technology to improve the performance of next generation data centres. The potential to develop Ethernet switches that exceed the performance of supercomputer networks gives the company high growth potential. In April 2008 Gnodal secured a £1.1m funding round from the YFM Group, South West Ventures Fund and NESTA. The market research company Dell 'Oro predicts that in 2011 the company's addressable market will be worth $4.8 billion.

Gnodal is a third generation Silicon South West company, in that the staff have 20 years sectoral and regional experience, having worked in Inmos, STMicroelectronics

and associated spin-offs in the region, such as Meiko and Quadrics. It is the concentration of such companies, and the accompanying support network that attracted Gnodal to locate in the area.

Gnodal is housed in the SETsquared incubator at Bristol University, and the agglomerated support services allowed the company to keep initial costs down and build a strong business case. Two of the founders, the CEO and Vice President of Marketing and Business Development, are alumni of Bristol and Bath Universities, and are maintaining links with the research base through Professor Alistair Munroe (Bristol University), an important relationship for the potential development of next generation technologies and further student recruitment.

Figure 6: Firms across the region

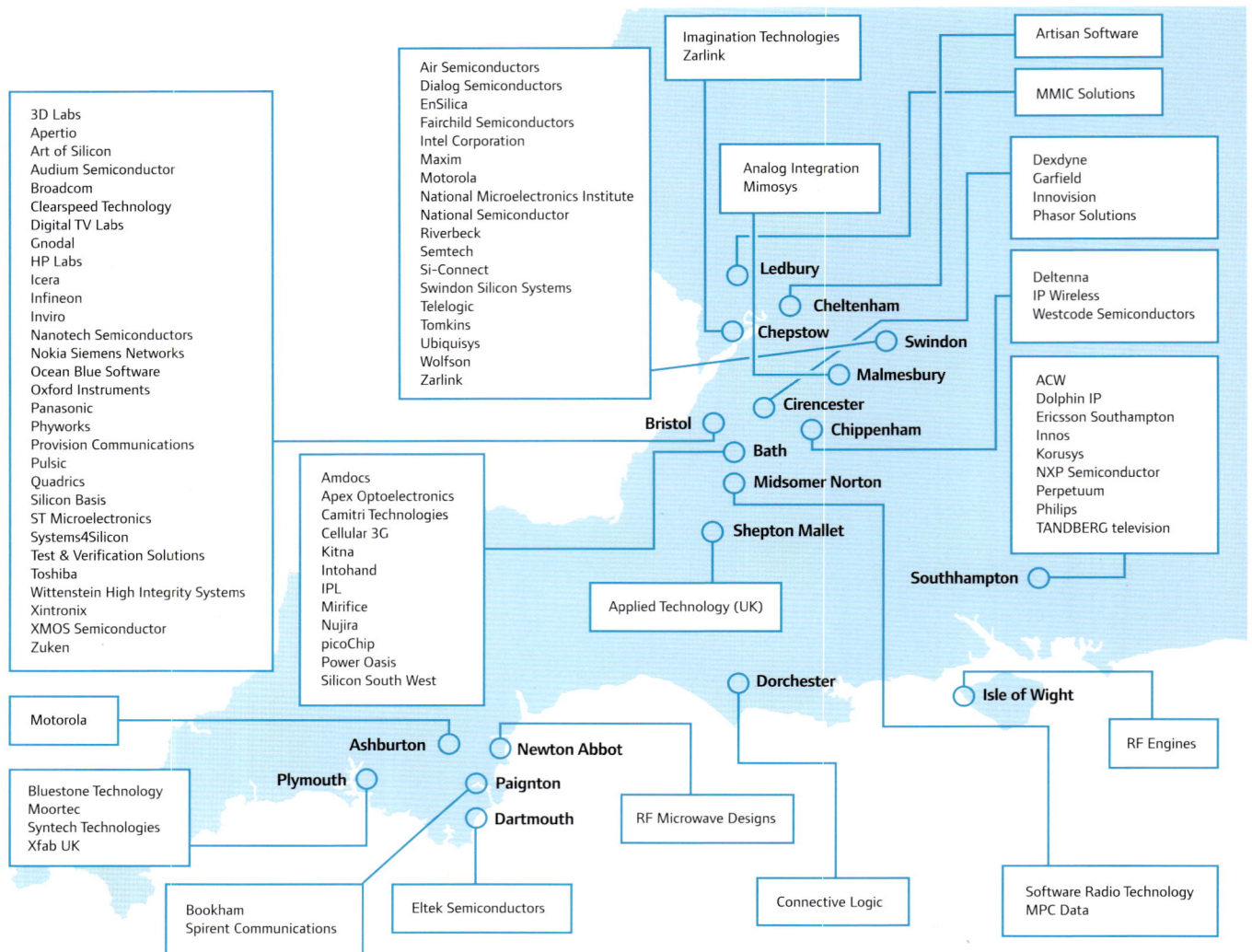

3D Labs
Apertio
Art of Silicon
Audium Semiconductor
Broadcom
Clearspeed Technology
Digital TV Labs
Gnodal
HP Labs
Icera
Infineon
Inviro
Nanotech Semiconductors
Nokia Siemens Networks
Ocean Blue Software
Oxford Instruments
Panasonic
Phyworks
Provision Communications
Pulsic
Quadrics
Silicon Basis
ST Microelectronics
Systems4Silicon
Test & Verification Solutions
Toshiba
Wittenstein High Integrity Systems
Xintronix
XMOS Semiconductor
Zuken

Air Semiconductors
Dialog Semiconductors
EnSilica
Fairchild Semiconductors
Intel Corporation
Maxim
Motorola
National Microelectronics Institute
National Semiconductor
Riverbeck
Semtech
Si-Connect
Swindon Silicon Systems
Telelogic
Tomkins
Ubiquisys
Wolfson
Zarlink

Imagination Technologies
Zarlink

Artisan Software

MMIC Solutions

Analog Integration
Mimosys

Dexdyne
Garfield
Innovision
Phasor Solutions

Ledbury

Cheltenham

Chepstow

Swindon

Malmesbury

Cirencester

Chippenham

Bristol

Bath

Midsomer Norton

Shepton Mallet

Deltenna
IP Wireless
Westcode Semiconductors

ACW
Dolphin IP
Ericsson Southampton
Innos
Korusys
NXP Semiconductor
Perpetuum
Philips
TANDBERG television

Southhampton

Amdocs
Apex Optoelectronics
Camitri Technologies
Cellular 3G
Kitna
Intohand
IPL
Mirifice
Nujira
picoChip
Power Oasis
Silicon South West

Applied Technology (UK)

Dorchester

Isle of Wight

RF Engines

Motorola

Bluestone Technology
Moortec
Syntech Technologies
Xfab UK

Ashburton

Newton Abbot

Plymouth

Paignton

Dartmouth

RF Microwave Designs

Connective Logic

Bookham
Spirent Communications

Eltek Semiconductors

Software Radio Technology
MPC Data

Source: Silicon South West, 2009.

Figure 7: Start-up investment and trade sales exits

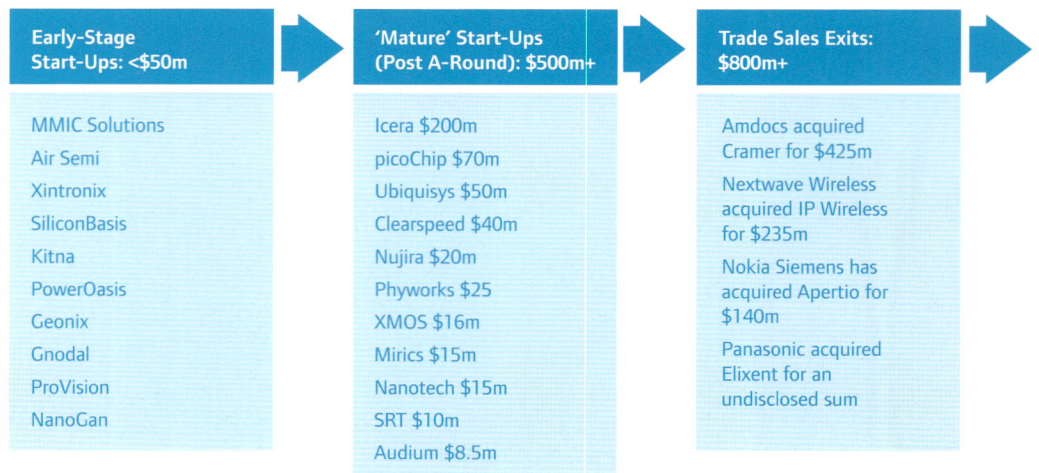

Early-Stage Start-Ups: <$50m	'Mature' Start-Ups (Post A-Round): $500m+	Trade Sales Exits: $800m+
MMIC Solutions	Icera $200m	Amdocs acquired Cramer for $425m
Air Semi	picoChip $70m	Nextwave Wireless acquired IP Wireless for $235m
Xintronix	Ubiquisys $50m	Nokia Siemens has acquired Apertio for $140m
SiliconBasis	Clearspeed $40m	Panasonic acquired Elixent for an undisclosed sum
Kitna	Nujira $20m	
PowerOasis	Phyworks $25	
Geonix	XMOS $16m	
Gnodal	Mirics $15m	
ProVision	Nanotech $15m	
NanoGan	SRT $10m	
	Audium $8.5m	

Source: Silicon South West, 2009.

Sheffield Hallam University: supporting regional growth in the creative industries

Regenerating Sheffield through growth of the creative industries

Sheffield Hallam University has played an important role in the development of the creative industries in Sheffield and South Yorkshire, as a collaborator in new initiatives and as a producer of human capital through a range of sector-specific courses. It demonstrates the role that new universities can play in local economic growth.

For decades Sheffield's economic fortune was dominated by heavy manufacturing. In the 1980s, in the face of severe international competition, the traditional regional industries of steel, cutlery and coal collapsed, with a loss of a quarter of all jobs in the city. Rebuilding and re-branding Sheffield became an urgent priority. As part of the response to this challenge, in 1988 Sheffield City Council embarked on a course of action to turn a derelict industrial area into a new growth hub for businesses in the emerging creative industries sector, known as the Cultural Industries Quarter (CIQ). Yorkshire Forward has also championed the transformation of Sheffield, with strategy to support the growth of knowledge-based regional clusters, including creative and digital industries, with 'universities at the heart of economic growth'.[53]

By 1998 the CIQ had become recognised as a leading centre for the creative industries, helping support regeneration. To consolidate this position and support further growth, in 1999 the CIQ Agency was formed, a partnership between the Council, Sheffield Hallam University (SHU) and businesses that had located there. In 2000 the first staff were appointed, to support growth of businesses, encourage private investment, champion the sector and build up the regional network.

Creativesheffield, a publicly funded City Development Company, also supports business innovation in the creative industries. Its 2008 economic master plan aims to support investment-marketing drives, infrastructure development and promote science and research across the sector. In March 2009, the Sheffield Digital Campus was opened, to provide office space and business support for start-up and early-stage companies. The £110 million e-Campus is supported by a range of public sector organisations and is closely located to SHU, as well as a transport hub. While there

is no formal link with SHU, it seems likely that many students and spin-outs will locate there.

Impacts

By 2005 over 9,000 people in 1,248 businesses were employed in Sheffield in the creative and digital industries, generating £700 million in turnover, equivalent to 9 per cent of the city's total.[54] Across the South Yorkshire region the sector employs in excess of 123,000 employees in more than 13,000 businesses – adding £5.21 billion gross value added to the region.[55] The region is home to many high performing home-grown businesses, such as The Designers Republic, Zoo Digital and Sumo, and international market leaders, for example AutoDesk, Ansys and OCLC.

It is predicted that the combined strength of the design, interactive media, mobile, ICT and healthcare technologies sectors will help create a further 4,000 jobs and 250 companies by 2015.[56]

SHU is an important partner in the creative industries cluster

In 2006/07 SHU received over £8.5 million in total collaborative income, £75,000 from IP. SHU generated four licences, but did not create any spin-outs, although it does have eight active spin-out companies.[57] However, SHU supports the development of the creative industries through other functions: it is a central partner in regional initiatives; and provides a range of courses and training that support the development of human capital, producing industry-skilled graduates.

The university is a central collaborator in regional initiatives

SHU has been involved in the growth of the creative industries sector over the last decade, as a stakeholder on the governing board of CIQA and as part of the Steering Group of the Digital Campus. Through its Enterprise Centre, co-located in the CIQ, SHU runs a number of knowledge transfer activities. Two hundred SMEs are assisted annually through consultancy projects and numerous national and international companies such as Braun, Philips, Pfizer, Marks and Spencer and the BBC have accessed specialist university expertise. In computing and IT there are strong links with SAP, Oracle, Microsoft and Cisco, supporting a range of product developments.[58]

SHU provides facilities and training for the creative industries

To improve the attractiveness of the location as a centre of excellence there has been an £81

53. Yorkshire Forward (2006) 'The Regional Economic Strategy 2006-2015.' Leeds: Yorkshire Forward.

54. Renaissance South Yorkshire (2007) 'South Yorkshire Creative & Digital Industries Study, Section 1 Performance & Potential 2000-2015.' Rotherham: Renaissance South Yorkshire.

55. Sheffield Digital Campus. See http://www.sheffielddigitalcampus.com/%20location/sheffield_facts_and_figures

56. Renaissance South Yorkshire (2007) 'South Yorkshire Creative & Digital Industries Study, Section 1 Performance & Potential 2000-2015.' Rotherham: Renaissance South Yorkshire.

57. HEFCE (2008) 'Higher education-business and community interaction survey: 2006–07.' Available at: http://www.hefce.ac.uk/pubs/hefce/2008/08_22/

58. For example, design and innovation consultancy for industry leaders including Coca-Cola, Umbro, Marks & Spencer and Britvic; work on advanced design of mobile technologies for rural workers in the Indian sub-continent, enabling workers to develop greater economic independence.

million investment in physical infrastructure, to provide learning and teaching facilities that can attract the best students. A similar amount has been earmarked for projects due for completion by 2010.[59]

SHU has established various new degrees tailored to meet the needs of the creative industries. Various undergraduate programmes such as the BA Games Design, BA Animation, BA Film and Visual Effects and BA Digital Media Production degrees enable a future generation of technical artists to use a vast resource of specialist expertise. More recently SHU launched an MSc entertainment software development course in association with Sony, to develop the expertise of graduates heading for careers in the industry. As a new university, the senior management is keen to reflect bottom-up approaches to teaching, with a majority of students on work placement and sandwich courses.

The combination of facilities, training and links across the region and with business makes SHU an attractive centre for creative industry students. Anecdotally, senior management in the university and Creativesheffield report that the strength of this package helps retain many students in the city and sector after they have graduated, a virtuous circle of growth.

Further initiatives to boost university-business interaction and innovation should be supported, such as the NESTA-HEFCE Creative Business Catalyst, a pilot programme that links MBA students to early-stage growth companies. The Manchester Masters is a similar scheme, bringing together students from all universities in the Manchester city-region with 60 businesses.[60]

Recognising and supporting the contribution of SHU to the regional economy

The university is strategically positioned according to Diana Green, former Vice Chancellor. "With its world-class provision in art and design, SHU is sandwiched geographically between the existing cultural industries quarter and the flagship e-campus project. It is key to the further development of the creative and digital industries cluster."[61]

One of the challenges for a university like Sheffield Hallam is quantifying – and being rewarded for – the economic contribution it makes. Its particular strengths are in the fields of place-making, 'knowledge exchange on legs', and developing links with local small businesses. University management argue that current HEIF metrics do not adequately reward these activities, leading academics to focus on more standard RAE goals. This raises the question of how well existing funding mechanisms address these wider economic development roles, especially for post-1992 universities.

59. Times Online (19 June 2008) 'Profile: Sheffield Hallam University.' Available at: http://www.timesonline.co.uk/tol/life_and_style/education/good_university_guide/article2166723.ece

The University of Dundee: excellence in life sciences

The University of Dundee has been and remains central to the development of a regional life sciences cluster. The combination of an excellent scientific base, novel but effective links to industry and the determination of strong leadership have driven this growth.

Dundee, located on the north bank of the Firth of Tay, has a population of approximately 140,000. Its economy, which was traditionally based on the manufacture of jute, has been transformed and it now has one of the leading life sciences clusters in the UK, with high-quality companies, research institutions and scientists. Currently more than 4,000 people work in Dundee's life sciences sector, which accounts for 16 per cent of the local economy,[62] with companies specialising in biotechnology, pharmaceuticals, medical devices and diagnostics. Some of these companies are described at the end of this case study.

The University of Dundee, in 2006/07, raised £1.2 million total income, almost entirely from IP revenue. The university filed 13 patents and generated 15 licences. It has 21 active spin-outs.[63] The success in commercial growth of the life sciences sector is based on the university's scientific excellence, spearheaded by a boundary-spanning leader and conducted through a novel form of university-business collaboration.

Scientific excellence and strong leadership in life sciences

The College of Life Sciences at the University of Dundee has a world-class reputation and it comprises over 760 researchers and support staff from 55 different countries. Research has shown that, between 1993 and 2003, 22 of the research team leaders were in the top 1 per cent most quoted scientists in their field, and in the areas of biology, biochemistry and genetics the university was either the first or the second most cited university in Europe – ahead of Cambridge, Oxford and University College London.[64]

One of its leading scientists is Professor Sir Philip Cohen who has undertaken pioneering research into protein phosphorylation, one of the body's main control systems which is co-ordinated by two classes of enzymes – protein phosphatases and protein kinases. Abnormalities in protein phosphorylation

are a cause of major diseases such as cancer, diabetes and rheumatoid arthritis and protein kinases have become the pharmaceutical industry's most important drug targets in the treatment of cancer or chronic inflammatory diseases.

A novel form of university-business collaboration

For 25 years there was little commercial interest in Cohen's research. It was only in the mid 1990s and with the development of a huge body of research, that the major pharmaceutical companies realised that they could now commercially exploit the work to create new drugs. This was partly due to the emergence of the drug Gleevec in the US, which is a potent kinase inhibitor, and has been successfully used in the treatment of some cancers. This stimulated interest in Cohen's research; he also realised that if he could establish an effective collaboration with the pharmaceutical companies he could acquire more resources that would strengthen the research of his group.

Cohen established a collaboration with a number of pharmaceutical companies that led to the formation of the Division of Signal Transduction Therapy (DSTT) at Dundee. This is a collaboration between scientists in the MRC Protein Phosphorylation Unit and the College of Life Sciences and six of the world's leading pharmaceutical companies (AstraZeneca, Boehringer Ingelheim, GlaxoSmithKline, Merck Co Inc, Merck KGaA and Pfizer). The collaboration aims to accelerate the development of specific inhibitors of kinases and phosphatases for the treatment of disease, as well the study of cell signalling.

Under the collaborative agreement the participating companies share access to the unpublished results, technology and know-how and they have the first rights to license the intellectual property the Division generates, but they pay extra for special services and to licence the IP. The Division does not carry out contract research as part of a collaborative arrangement. Sixty per cent of the budget is spent on basic research projects and the remainder is spent on providing the services for the participating companies which also are very valuable for the unit's research. Scientists from the participating companies visit the unit in Dundee three times a year for presentations of the latest results and to discuss areas of mutual interest. The University of Dundee received a Queen's Anniversary Award in 2006 in recognition of the contributions of the DSTT,

60. See http://www.manchestermasters.com
61. Diana Green. 'Guardian' 11 March, 2003.
62. See http://www.biodundee.co.uk
63. HEFCE (2008) 'Higher education-business and community interaction survey: 2006–07.' Available at: http://www.hefce.ac.uk/pubs/hefce/2008/08_22/
64. See Dundee University website (2003). Available at: http://www.dundee.ac.uk/pressreleases/praug03/citation.html

which has become a model for knowledge exchange between the academic and business communities.

Clusters of scientific and commercial should be built on regional strengths

The consortium of companies that support the work of Sir Philip Cohen shows the importance of aligning interests: the pharmaceutical companies benefit as the collaboration speeds up drug discovery; the academics benefit as the collaboration provides more resources for research. It also shows the importance of novel forms of knowledge exchange that depend on long-term relationships. The consortium model is important as it would have been unlikely that a single company would have supported the research programme which is high-risk, uncertain and has unpredictable time scales. Furthermore, it shows the importance of committed and talented people, the collaboration would not have started without both the scientific excellence and perseverance of Sir Philip Cohen.

Examples of businesses operating in the Dundee life sciences cluster

CXR Biosciences: Spun-out from the university in 2001, they employ 40 staff. The company supplies a range of products and services aimed at accelerating drug discovery processes. It is headed up by Dr Tom Shepherd – Chair of Scotland's Life Sciences Alliance. CXR won the UK Trade & Investment's UK Innovation Enabling Biotechnology Award in 2006.

Cypex: Spun-out in 1999, they employ five staff. University research was a product of a partnership involving 15 pharmaceutical companies. Company products are used in drug development labs to predict the way new drugs will be broken down in the human body.

Cyclacel: Spun-out in 1996 and has 60 staff. It is a drug discovery, development and commercialisation business, focused on human cancers and other serious disorders. They have a series of linkups with larger drug companies including GlaxoSmithKline and AstraZeneca.

Axis-Shield: Spun-out in 1982, they employ 120 staff. The company produces products for laboratory and surgery use in cardiovascular disease, rheumatoid arthritis, infectious diseases and diabetes.

Open innovation at Daresbury

The thriving high-tech cluster around the Daresbury Laboratory in Cheshire shows how national research facilities can play a similar role to research universities as economic anchors. This is an approach that could usefully be emulated at other similar sites.

Daresbury introduced a new system of business support based on the concept of 'open innovation', which has helped maximise the commercial exploitation of the 'big science' projects taking place there. The laboratory has invested to build strong networks between research, business and academia that have increased its ability to generate start-ups and support economic growth.

The Daresbury Laboratory has been a world-class centre for big science since 1962, with seven large-scale facilities housing leading-edge research and experimentation in areas such as accelerator science, synchrotron light exploitation, advanced engineering and nuclear physics.

In 2005 the Northwest Regional Development Agency (NWDA) and European Regional Development Fund invested £50 million to build a Science and Innovation Campus, intended to improve the innovation system at Daresbury and so maximise public investment in science on business innovation.[65]

The Campus is based on an open innovation model that encourages collaboration and knowledge exchange intended to accelerate the process of technological commercialisation. It is jointly governed by the Science & Technology Facilities Council (STFC), NWDA, Lancaster University, University of Liverpool, University of Manchester and Halton Borough Council. The co-location of academics, scientists, businesses and business support services helps create a critical mass of world-class science, high quality skills and industry. This model is demonstrating impact on the regional economy.

Impacts
Eighty-five Daresbury companies, in fields such as healthcare, digital/ICT and energy technologies, have delivered £14.9 million per year in sales in the last financial year, and secured £20.5 million of investment to date. Sales have grown by 67 per cent in the last year. Three-quarters of companies have developed new products and services, of which two-thirds of them have been taken to market. Daresbury companies have created 64 full-time employment jobs this year. Of the £20.5 million funding raised to date, £7.3 million was in the last year, a 55 per cent increase on the previous year. Of the total amount, 47 per cent was venture capital funding, albeit with £6 million to one company.[66]

Creating a Science and Innovation Campus
To create the Campus, a number of new centres were built, including the Daresbury Innovation Centre and the Cockroft Institute.

The Cockcroft Institute is the UK centre for accelerator science. It is a joint venture between STFC scientists and the Universities of Lancaster, Liverpool and Manchester, creating a critical mass of intelligence alongside the essential scientific and technological facilities for research and development.

The Innovation Centre offers a range of business services and office and laboratory space to support the growth of high-tech SME businesses. The Centre encourages interaction between companies (blue chips and SMEs), the research, science and skills base of the stakeholder universities, the STFC, and public sector business support services (such as the NWDA, Halton Borough Council, UK Trade and Investment (UKTI) and Business Link).

More recently, the IDEAS partnership, a consortium of business schools from Lancaster, Liverpool and Manchester universities, has been established at Daresbury to provide innovative management-focused research, advice and training to firms to further strengthen support and collaboration on the campus and beyond.

Encouraging collaboration is a major part of the Daresbury experiment
Seventy-three per cent of companies collaborate with each other, 50 per cent with the STFC and stakeholder universities. Companies frequently share opportunities to pitch to potential external investment sources, for example 12 companies recently presented to the British Airports Authority, with three invited to submit more details.

About half of the companies use Business Link and UKTI services. Those companies with a 'supernetworker', or someone that collaborates with other companies, the STFC and the university, have higher than average sales growth (106 per cent in 2008 and 185 per cent in 2007). Businesses tend to collaborate with the university for technical support and student recruitment. Physical proximity and co-

65. HM Treasury (2006) 'Science and innovation investment framework 2004-2014: next steps.' London: HM Treasury.
66. Daresbury Science and Innovation Campus (2009) '2008 Tenants Survey.' Daresbury: Daresbury Science and Innovation Campus.

location facilitates R&D linkages and access to technology transfer opportunities. A networked approach supports business access to new markets or customers and to capital networks.[67]

Focused around the Innovation Centre, the Campus offers a neutral space to build a network between business, entrepreneurs, academia and scientists, supported by essential facilities and support staff. Currently, there is a network of 1,500 and growing at about 500 people per year. Network interactions are managed to strategically connect the right people to each other, for example through targeted monthly business breakfasts which typically attract about 130-140 people from across the network.

Networks provide intelligence and support that help companies grow, such as guidance on developing the right routes to market, the skills to deliver commercialisation, marketing and product placement.

A growing regional hub
The creation of an innovative science and enterprise cluster has had positive effects on the North West economy and Daresbury has big plans for site expansion, with huge economic potential predicted.

£65 million investment has been allocated from the DIUS Large Facilities Capital Fund to create two new technology gateway centres – Hartree (computational science) and Detector Systems, and Vanguard House will create more space for new and larger companies. The vision for the next 25 to 30 years is to create a Technology Village of 15,000 people across 300 hectares, with new housing and an improved transport infrastructure (see Figure 8). Estimates suggest that £600 million investment over the next 30 years could create 12,000 new jobs on-site producing an additional £217 million gross value added to the regional economy.[68]

Supporting the successful growth of Daresbury
Open innovation at Daresbury has stimulated cross-sectoral and interdisciplinary interactions that have helped to build an internationally recognised community of scientific, innovation and entrepreneurial excellence.

To ensure continued growth, one challenge is to expand the network and build up the critical mass. Brokerage will be required to maintain on-going partnerships and secure new, wider partnerships. Nascent government plans to create a structure that can co-ordinate the range of Daresbury approaches into a wider outreach package should be consolidated and implemented.[69] Greater online presence would also support this aim.

The development of Daresbury has been well supported to date, through government policy and strong leadership. The efforts of individuals such as Lord Sainsbury and Colin Whitehouse have helped steer a common vision. The joint governance structure has eased the planning process for site expansion. The early buy-in from local authorities, notably the financial commitment of the NWDA, has helped convert the vision into a reality.

Although Daresbury is not itself a university, it provides an important lesson in how to capitalise on research excellence. Daresbury not only encourages spin-outs and licensing, but it has invested in the infrastructure necessary to encourage the emergence of a cluster, both physical (in the form of its campus) and social (by encouraging supernetworkers and providing a range of business services). Plans are now in train to extend the Daresbury model to its sister STFC 'dipole' site at Harwell and the Rutherford Appleton Laboratory, (near Oxford) to help stimulate collaboration, networking and spin-outs at this major research hub as well. These developments, together with emerging hubs at King's Cross (site of a new London medical campus) and Longbridge (site of a technology park), are potentially important drivers of economic growth, supporting linkages from the knowledge base to business, generating technological innovations that can attract investment.

67. Ibid.
68. Manchester Independent Economic Review (2009) 'Review of Daresbury Science and Innovation Campus.' Available at: http://www.manchester-review.org.uk/
69. Plans include a new joint venture company, the appointment of a Science Champion and the launch of the Knowledge Centre for Material Chemistry. See DIUS press release (26 March 2009) 'Government renews its commitment to Daresbury.' Available at: http://www.dius.gov.uk/news_and_speeches/press_releases/daresbury

Figure 8: Daresbury campus vision – a 30 year master plan

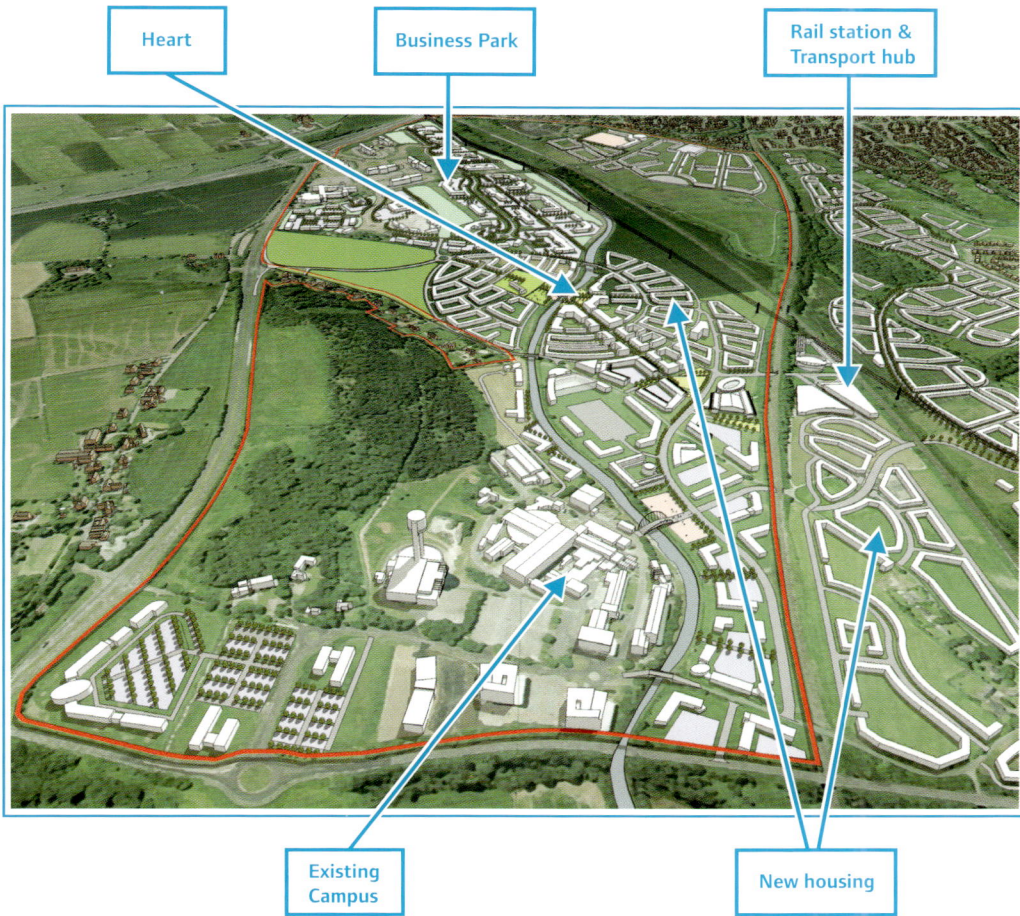

Heart

Business Park

Rail station & Transport hub

Existing Campus

New housing

Part 3: The changing face of university-business interactions

70. HEIF Rounds 1, 2 and 3. See http://www.hefce.ac.uk/econsoc/buscom/heif/heif.asp

One clear message from our case studies is the increasing importance of universities' contribution to the economy and the outside world. It is particularly revealing to look at how this role has changed over time, and how it appears to be evolving now.

We would argue that the UK's universities are mid-way through a journey from a state of relative isolation from the wider economy, to a more deeply involved relationship. At one time, universities existed in what might be characterised as a state of 'serendipity', where connections with the outside economy occurred sporadically and occasionally – if at all. Over the past decade, universities have increased and systematised their ability to protect and profit from their intellectual property, strengthening and professionalising their technology transfer and consulting capabilities. We might call this intermediate model 'the commercial university', since it is considerably more open to business and innovation than the 'serendipitous university' model.

However, the journey does not stop there: the challenge now is for universities to systematise and scale up their other interactions with businesses in the same way they have done in relation to patents and licences. The successes of Southampton, Daresbury and the South West in developing a much broader set of interactions with businesses, attracting foreign investment and helping regional economic clusters and innovation systems to flourish, demonstrate how it is possible to develop formal and informal interaction, including but not limited to technology transfer. We call this model 'the connected university'. In the section that follows we explain this evolution and the implications for the future development of universities' interaction with businesses.

The Serendipitous University model: happenstance and good fortune

Traditionally, universities focussed on two missions – research and education. The knowledge generated in many universities did contribute to the local economy and innovation system but this was sporadic and driven by processes of serendipity, chance, luck or historical circumstance. The 'Cambridge Phenomenon' is frequently cited as an example of the impact that a university can have on its local economy and the development of a high technology cluster, but as we have argued this evolved through serendipity and luck.

The success of Cambridge's approach arguably has more to do with the sheer weight of valuable knowledge that the university generated than the effectiveness of its early approach to business interaction.

The Commercial University model – taking science and technology transfer seriously

During the past 15 years the UK government has increasingly focussed on the ways that universities influence competitiveness and innovation. Much of this focus has concentrated on the commercialisation of technology (such as spin-outs, patents and licences) and science entrepreneurship. Initiatives such as the Science Enterprise Challenge and the early rounds of the Higher Education Innovation Fund (HEIF) focussed on developing 'closer links between HEIs, public sector research organisations and industry, leading to greater exploitation of science'.[70]

Encouraging the Commercial University

The focus on commercialising science has stimulated a significant growth in the number of technology transfer offices since the 1990s.[71] There were nearly 6,000 more staff working in technology transfer and industrial liaison in 2006/7 compared to six years earlier, as shown in Table 3. The growing demand for specialists in technology transfer stimulated new training schemes to provide the necessary skills. For example, Praxis is a national training programme for technology transfer professionals working in universities, research institutions and business. Praxis was spun-out from the Cambridge-MIT Institute (CMI) and it origins can be traced to concerns raised through CMI's National Competitiveness Network that while technology transfer was becoming more important, the UK lacked the appropriate skills in this area. In addition to providing support staff, there has been modest help to help finance commercialisation. The University Challenge Fund (UCF) launched in 1998 enabled universities to access seed funding to help the commercialisation of university intellectual property.

The objective of stimulating entrepreneurship was reflected in the Science Enterprise Challenge, which established a network of centres in UK universities which specialised in the teaching and practice of commercialisation and science-based entrepreneurship. Additionally, the National Council for Graduate Entrepreneurship was formed in 2004 with the objective of raising the profile of entrepreneurship as a career choice amongst students and graduates.

The Higher Education Innovation Fund is a programme designed to encourage knowledge exchange in universities and other higher education institutions in England (the devolved assemblies of Scotland, Wales and Northern Ireland have their own support mechanisms). An analysis of the HEIF programme shows that it is seen as extremely important in 51 per cent of English universities as it helps to stimulate collaborations that would otherwise be too costly to develop, encourages culture change and a strategic focus on knowledge exchange.[72] HEIF has evolved through its four rounds, not only through its funding formulas, but also it has increasingly adopted a wider view of the role of university-business interactions. The first round in 2001 aimed to develop: "closer links between HEIs, public sector research organisations and industry, leading to greater exploitation of science".[73] But by the fourth round in 2008, the objective was "to support

and develop a broad range of knowledge transfer activities which result in economic and social benefit to the UK, [providing incentives] for higher education institutions (HEIs) to work with business, public sector bodies and third sector".[74]

Support for the commercial university model is now well established. There is emerging support from public policy for the wider dimensions of university-business interactions. But this support needs to be developed and made more systematic.

This model has stimulated economic growth

Evidence about the extent of interactions between universities and business is collected through the Higher Education – Business Community Interaction (HE-BCI) surveys (see Table 3). These data show that the number of patents applied for and granted has more than doubled between 2000/1 and 2006/7. During the same period, the number of licences has more than quadrupled and annual income from licensing intellectual property tripled from £18 million to £58 million.

Between 1994 and 1999 there were 338 spin-outs, an average of 70 per year. By 2006/07, 226 companies spun out of universities in just one year. From 2001 to 2007 the total turnover of all active university spin-outs increased by 240 per cent, and between 2004 and 2007, 25 spin-outs from UK universities floated on stock exchanges. These companies raised over £250 million from the capital markets at the initial public offering stage and have a market capitalisation of more than £1.5 billion.[75] (The fall in the number of spin-outs between 2003–05 reflects taxation changes and difficulties in raising finance for high technology start-ups during this period.)

Overall, the focus on making the commercialisation of intellectual property more systematic has yielded benefits to the UK. The spin-out companies described in the Southampton and South West case studies are good examples of this.

Limitations of the Commercial University model

But, as noted earlier, the interaction between businesses and universities involves more than just the transfer of intellectual property. University interactions with business include a wide spectrum of activities with multiple 'pathways', 'channels', 'processes' or 'linking mechanisms'. Increasing the stock of codified knowledge is only one type of interaction

71. Lambert, R. (2003) 'Lambert Review of university-business collaboration. Final Report.' London: HM Treasury.

72. PACEC (2008) 'Analysis of HEIF 4 institutional strategies.' Report to HEFCE. Cambridge: PACEC.

73. HEFCE (2001) 'Higher Education Innovation Fund Invitation to apply for special funding, Annex A Knowledge Exploitation Funding: guidance notes.' Bristol: HEFCE.

74. HEFCE (2008b) 'Higher Education Innovation Fund Round 4: invitation and guidance for institutional strategies. Bristol: HEFCE.

75. Lord Sainsbury of Turville (2007) 'Race to the top: A Review of Government's Science and Innovation Policies.' London: HM Treasury.

Table 3: Higher Education – Business Community Interaction Survey Indicators (HEFCE)

Indicator	2000/01	2001/02	2002/03	2003/04	2004/05	2005/06	2006/07
Number of new patents filed by Higher Education Institute	896	960	1,222	1,308	1,649	1,537	1,913
Number of patents granted	250	198	377	463	711	576	647
Number of licensing agreements	728	615	758	2,256	2,099	2,699	3,286
Income from licensing intellectual property (£ million)	18	47	37	38	57	58	58
Number of spin-outs	248	213	197	161	148	187	226
Income from business (value of consultancy contracts) (£ millions)	104	122	168	211	219	236	288
Number of full-time equivalent staff employed in commercialisation /industrial liaison offices	1,538	1,836	2,283	2,706	3,077	3,448	7,440

Source: Higher Education – Business Community Interaction (HE-BCI) data quoted in HM Treasury (2008) 'Science and Innovation Investment Framework 2004 – 2014: annual report 2008'. London: HM Treasury and DIUS, Table 3.1.

76. Lester, R. (2005) 'Universities, Innovation, and the Competitiveness of Local Economies: A Summary Report from the Local Innovation Systems Project— Phase I.' MIT Industrial Performance Center Working Paper 05-010. Cambridge, MA: MIT.

77. Hughes, A. (2008) Innovation policy as cargo cult: myth and reality in knowledge- led productivity growth. In Bessant, J. and Venables, T. (Eds) 'Creating Wealth from Knowledge. Meeting the Innovation Challenge.' Cheltenham: Edward Elgar.

78. Times Higher Education article (10 July 2008) 'Intellectual property investment of £20m yields just 1% fillip in income.' Available at: http://www.timeshighereducation.co.uk/story.asp?storyCode=40268 7&sectioncode=26

79. Targeting Innovation (2008) 'Scottish University Spin-out study June 08.' Glasgow: Targeting Innovation.

80. Abreu, M., Grinevich, V., Kitson, M. and Savona, M. (2007) 'Absorptive Capacity and Regional Patterns of Innovation.' London: DIUS; Salter, A. and Tether, B. (2006) 'Innovation in Services through the Looking Glass of Innovation Studies.' Advanced Institute of Management (AIM) Background Paper for the AIM Grand Challenge on Service Science, April 2006, AIM, London.

81. Abreu, M., Grinevich, V., Kitson, M. and Savona, M. (2008) 'Taking services seriously: How policymakers can stimulate the 'hidden innovation' in the UK's service economy.' London: NESTA.

82. BDI report 'Delivering the Innovation Dream.' Commissioned by DIUS

at the university-business interface. Others include the traditional role of educating people, problem-solving such as contract and co-operative research, and public space functions such as informal social interactions, meetings and conferences.[76]

Indeed, the gains from technology transfer alone can be over-estimated and are often skewed, with a few big hits generating much of the income, and many technology transfer offices may take considerable time before they cover their costs.[77] The generation of intellectual property is important for economic growth – particularly in the long-term – as many technologies that have their origins in university research can lead to productivity gains. But many of these gains are often due to the diffusion of technologies and the impacts of spillovers, where the benefits are not directly captured by those that originally developed the technology. As an advisor to the CBI observed: "Like DNA, most IP is junk. Obviously, some of it is extremely important and extremely valuable, but in order to get the full benefit of the extremely important stuff a lot of investment has to be made."[78]

It is also possible that a focus on a narrow range of metrics involving patents and licensing may distort behaviour, encouraging the generation of patents and licences when other forms of knowledge exchange may be more appropriate.[79]

The focus on a technology transfer approach fails to capture the full range of university-business interactions. In particular focusing on science, technology and engineering fails to account for the many contributions from other disciplines.[80] For instance research has shown the importance of interactions between business and the social sciences which are especially important for innovation in the service sector.[81]

At the other extreme, concerns have been raised over the effect of university consulting activities on the fortunes of small professional services firms, such as design businesses.[82] This can be overcome by ensuring that universities treat their consulting activities as genuinely economic propositions, avoiding long-term cross-subsidies from teaching and infrastructure funds, but is an important unintended consequence to guard against.

The Connected University model – the wider dimensions of university-business interactions
Our case studies show that successful universities are increasingly focusing on a much wider range of interactions with business. They are taking the systematic approach that has

historically been applied to technology transfer, and building on this to improve their ability to nurture clusters, to develop the workforce of local businesses, and to build innovative networks from which local businesses (whether spin-outs or multinationals) can benefit.

The wider and more extensive role of universities in the innovation ecosystem was first highlighted in the Sainsbury Review (2007), stressing the importance of both their basic and applied research. The 'Innovation Nation' White Paper on Innovation focuses on universities as part of the 'innovation system' where innovation is a complex non-linear process. The Annual Innovation Report 2008 argues that:

> "Government's ambition is to build on the UK's world-class research base and to broaden the traditional knowledge exchange agenda to encompass new disciplines, new sectors, new businesses and those who work in the development and delivery of public services."

The wider framework is also reflected in the latest round of HEIF funding – HEIF 4 "is designed to support and develop a broad range of knowledge exchange activities which will result in economic and social benefit to the UK".

Support for a broader spectrum of university-business interactions is reflected to some extent in existing policy. In particular, Knowledge Transfer Partnerships (KTP) and their predecessor, the Teaching Company Scheme (TCS), are programmes to improve business competitiveness and productivity by facilitating partnerships between academia and business. KTPs establish relationships between companies and an academic institution to facilitate the transfer of knowledge, technology and skills. KTPs are now managed by the Technology Strategy Board and involve 437 departments in 102 Universities and nearly 1,000 businesses.[83]

This breadth is important. The Connected University model applies not only to traditionally research-oriented universities, but to all universities, and indeed to Further Education Colleges. Interaction with local businesses, whether in the form of consulting, informal links, or support for local economic development, can provide a source of valuable input to universities' teaching and other academic roles, as well as providing a valuable local economic benefit. Knowledge exchange

extends beyond the commercial exploitation of cutting-edge research by high-tech businesses. It can involve using established research knowledge in new ways or with new users, as well as interactions where the transfer is through consultancy, secondment, tailored training programmes, design input and technology or equipment-sharing rather than research. This broader range of interaction can be particularly important for small or less technologically sophisticated businesses.

The Connected University: issues to address
However, we believe universities can do more to become actively involved with businesses beyond the world of technology transfer. There are five main areas where there is room for more work from universities, business and policymakers.

1. There are low levels of interaction with small and medium-sized businesses
The allure of small, high-growth firms based on university IP is powerful and attractive. But we should not overlook the fact that most small businesses find it hard to exploit the benefits of working with universities. They often lack specialised staff with the time and knowledge to build links with academics, or to spend time assessing opportunities. Universities can play a role by making their work more open to businesses, and encouraging firms to interact with relevant researchers. Achieving good university-SME links is certainly possible; in Italy research shows that university research promotes the concentration of SMEs both in high-tech and other sectors.[84]

2. Many collaborations are not measured in existing metrics
Technology transfer usually has tangible, measurable benefits, such as capital raised by spin-outs or patents registered. Informal knowledge exchange, and the impact of universities in building clusters, are harder to capture in a single metric. The risk is that the lack of comparability leads to a lack of accountability and effectiveness. The challenge here is to measure what can be measured, and set realistic (even if qualitative) plans for the rest, to ensure that resources are not wasted on low-impact schemes.

3. A lack of boundary-spanning skills
Promoting better networks and building clusters requires a set of wider skills and perspectives than might traditionally exist in many university departments. These skills need to be developed, just as technology transfer skills needed to be learned when Technology

83. DIUS (2008) 'Annual Innovation Report 2008.' London: DIUS.
84. Rodríguez-Pose, A. and Refolo, M. (2000) 'The Link Between Clusters of SMEs and Public and University Research in Italy.' Paper presented to the 40th European Congress of the International Regional Science Associations, Barcelona.

Transfer Offices were set up. Newcastle's approach, appointing Professors of Practice, gives an example of how this might be achieved.

4. A lack of business demand

Analysis of the HEIF programme shows that wider external collaborations that would otherwise be too costly to develop encourage culture change and a strategic focus on knowledge exchange.[85] The Lambert Review, notes that the problem of university-business interaction come down in part to businesses' limited demand for interacting with universities.

> "The main challenge for the UK is not about how to increase the supply of commercial ideas from the universities into business. Instead, the question is about how to raise the overall level of demand by business for research from all sources."[86]

In some cases, this lack of demand may be because there are no benefits to be gained from collaboration. In some, however, it is because the process of interacting with the university is unnecessarily difficult or the benefits are not well understood.

5. Relationships between universities and business need active management

Barriers between business and universities are rising as businesses are frustrated with university bureaucracy and the 'unrealistic expectations' of universities about how much research discoveries are worth.[87] The evidence shows a significant rise in barriers between 2004 and 2008 with over 50 per cent of businesses citing potential conflicts with regards to intellectual property and regulations imposed by universities or government as being very important or crucial barriers to interaction in 2008. Furthermore, the most important barriers in 2008 were the long-term orientation of university research and the lack of suitable government programmes to support interactions. The misalignment of time frames, with business seeking quicker results than universities, reflects their different missions – business being driven by profits and shareholder value and universities driven by discovering new knowledge. Attempting to address this barrier, particularly by speeding up the research process in universities could damage one of the central missions, and the competitive advantage, of universities.

Some leading academics have remarked on the danger of universities becoming dependent upon commercialisation of research findings and becoming proprietary performers of R&D.[88] This would threaten the open science model that has historically been effective for the conduct of fundamental research and the discovery of knowledge. Also, the level of concern of businesses about the long-term orientation of universities has more than doubled between 2004 and 2008 – and this may reflect the different economic conditions when the surveys were undertaken. As the economy was entering recession in 2008, businesses may have shifted their focus to short-term business performance and survival and not the long-term benefits of interactions with universities. We must ensure that economic conditions do not distract universities and businesses from vital opportunities for long-term grants and collaborations.

85. PACEC (2008) 'Analysis of HEIF 4 institutional strategies.' Report to HEFCE. Cambridge: PACEC.

86. HM Treasury (2003) 'Lambert Review of university-business collaboration.' London: HM Treasury.

87. Bruneel, J., D'Este, P., Neely, A. and Salter, A. (2009) 'The Search for Talent and Technology: Examining the attitudes of EPSRC industrial collaborators towards universities.' London: Advanced Institute of Management Research.

88. David, P. and Metcalfe, S. (2008) 'Only Connect: Academic-Business Research Collaborations and the Formation of Ecologies of Innovation.' Stanford Institute for Economic Policy Research, SIEPR Discussion Paper No. 07-33. Stanford: Stanford Institute for Economic Policy Research.

Part 4: Policy recommendations

The future direction for policy

The past decade has seen a significant improvement in the way that universities translate their insights into economic impact, driven by the professionalisation of technology transfer and the availability of venture funding.

Over the coming years, universities will face increased demands to demonstrate the wider economic value they create, not least as science and technology research funding remains protected amid widespread spending cuts. With this in mind, it is in universities' interests to build a strong case for their wider social benefit, not least their impacts in delivering economic growth.

Getting the basics right

The first prerequisite for a university to make a strong economic contribution is to ensure that it has absorbed the lessons of the 'commercial university'. Policies should ensure that technology transfer organisations in universities match up, where applicable, to the standard set by leaders, such as Cambridge and Manchester in the larger research-intensive universities or 'good practice' initiatives in the wider pool of pre- and post-1992 institutions, such as Sheffield Hallam. Minimum size of unit may be an issue here and consideration needs to be given as to how universities may combine their resources in technology transfer to provide a more effective service in the field of knowledge exchange and commercialisation.

The importance of building innovation networks

Once this has been achieved, the university should ensure it focuses on building the wider networks required to work effectively with a wide range of businesses. The exchange of knowledge, cross-sectoral collaborations and interdisciplinary research have been shown to be essential to the innovation process in all the case studies. The impacts generated through building up and exploiting a critical mass of excellence is evident. But this exchange can take time and be difficult and costly – and most importantly it needs the building of communities which include businesses, academics and policymakers working together and developing long-term relationships, spaces where networks are encouraged to grow. To help support physical building it is important that planning and transport policies act to support regional growth, especially in clusters of scientific, research and commercial excellence, as described in Daresbury and Southampton, and applicable to Harwell and the recently announced King's Cross medical cluster.[89]

Networks require links not only between sectors, departments and institutions but also within them. There is an emerging evidence base on creating such linkages. NESTA is trialling innovative interdisciplinary approaches in its Crucible programme, bringing together a range of researchers and in turn generating new opportunities for collaboration and research exploitation. The success of this model is being replicated in Scotland. The Technology Strategy Board adopts a similar 'sand box' approach for its platforms. Policy should continue to support experimental and innovative ways that help create linkages between institutions and between individuals.

Universities should develop new skills in their staff and encourage boundary-spanners

There has been a significant and important increase in the number of technology transfer specialists working in universities in the past

89. The Government's Medical Research Council (MRC) has joined forces with the Wellcome Trust, Cancer Research UK and University College, London (UCL) to develop the £350 million British Library International Science Site (Bliss). It is intended to be the largest laboratory of its kind in the world, accommodating 1,500 leading researchers in different fields.

decade, with evidence of success in Cambridge, Southampton, Dundee and Manchester.

Although there are good examples of effective knowledge exchange in the UK, there is a need for more effective institutions and processes to facilitate the interactions between universities and business. The process of knowledge exchange should be addressed no less seriously than the traditional field of technology transfer.

Universities should earmark development funding to train both administrative and (some) research staff in how to build links with businesses, following the example of the Institute of Knowledge Transfer and the Leadership Foundation for Higher Education's HE and Civic Leadership programme, and encouraging more business placements for graduate students and researchers. Time spent in industry should be valued for academic career advancement purposes, and more information made available to researchers on options for working with businesses. Multi-disciplinary research within universities will also be important, as many of the most industrially valuable fields of expertise transcend traditional faculty boundaries. Universities should implement schemes based on NESTA's Crucible programme to develop these important internal connections. Universities should also consider emulating Newcastle in appointing senior outsiders to positions where they can increase university-business links.

Current measures proposed by some Vice-Chancellors and research councils to tackle the recession, in particular those that involve funding new graduate employees to work part-time while undertaking technical masters degrees to reduce graduate unemployment, could help shape the next generation of boundary-spanners.

Planning systems must support collaboration

The Daresbury and Sheffield case studies show the importance of shared spaces in developing university-business collaboration and boosting the economic benefits of universities. But as the Southampton example shows, the application of planning policy can get in the way in practice. Local authorities should ensure their planning systems give appropriate weight to the benefits of business-research co-location, and support them through appropriate transport and infrastructure policy.

Collaboration must be effectively measured and rewarded

University and research funding structures are currently under review: HEFCE is developing the Research Excellence Framework (REF) and the future versions of the Higher Education Innovation Fund. This provides a number of opportunities for government to support universities' interaction with the wider economy. It also underlines the need to improve how we measure these benefits.

The next version of HEIF should include broader measures of economic and social impact; at present it is acknowledged to be an imperfect proxy since it mainly focuses on outside revenue, rather than income or wider value creation. In the meantime, the HEIF model of funding should be extended to Further Education Colleges. 'FEIF', as it might be called, would encourage Further Education institutions to develop their interactions with local businesses and ensure that success in this area was recognised and rewarded.

There is also a case for using the REF to strengthen incentives for university-business collaboration. Existing good practice, such as the Medical Research Councils' industry collaboration awards or the BBSRC's industrial partnerships awards, could be built on, with a larger proportion of research councils' funding being dedicated to such programmes.

Regardless of whether funding mechanisms change, there is an urgent need to improve the metrics that universities use to gauge their broader relationships with business. If universities are to professionalise their network-building role in the same way we have professionalised their technology transfer role, they need to be able to measure performance. Alongside spin-outs and patents, we need to develop ways to measure and assess university-business exchange of staff, joint research, cluster size and stability, and the impact of interdisciplinary work.